Who Let This Guy in the White House?
by
Rod Warren

Featuring:
The Rebubbacans
and
The Autocrats

Illustrations by
Rod Warren

List of Characters
Donald Trumpet-President
Melonia Trumpet-Wife of Donald Trumpet
Jared Kushyner-Trumpet's Son-in-Law
Michael Pensive-Vice President
Steve Cannon-Trumpet's Chief Strategist
Cory Looseandrowsy-Trumpet's Campaign Manager
Dave Bossy-Trumpet's Deputy Campaign Manager
Paul Manthefort-Trumpet's Convention Campaign Mgr.
Carder Page-Trumpet Campaign Volunteer
George Papacropolis-Trumpet Campaign Volunteer
Johnny D.-Assistant & Counselor to Trumpet
Michael Flinn-National Security Advisor
Peter Navarho-President's Assistant
Prince Riebus-Chief of Staff
General John Killy-Chief of Staff
Andy McCave-Deputy Director of FBI
Rodney Rotenstein-Deputy Attorney General
Sean Spicey-Press Secretary
Sarah Huckleberry Sanders-Press Secretary
Jeff Sayshuns-Attorney General
Jim Comby-FBI Director
John Brinen-Director of the CIA
James Claptrapper-Director of National Unintelligence
Streter Pzok-FBI Chief of Counterespionage
Leesa Page-FBI attorney
Nancy Lugosi-Autocratic House Leader
Chuck Shoemer-Autocratic Senate Leader
Mitch McColonel-Rebubbacan Senate Leader
Robert Muller-Russia Investigation Special Counselor
Buhrock Obahma-Incumbent President
Joe Hiden -Incumbent Vice President
Hillery Clinkton-Incumbent Secretary of State

Rebubbacan Senators:
John Kinadee
Ted Caruzo

Autocratic Senators:
Borey Cooker
Bernie Slanders

Rebubbacan Representatives:
Liz Chainy
Rand Pall

Autocratic Representatives:
Adam Shifty
Jerry Madler
Eric Swallowell
Maxcine Wahwahs
Elizabeth Warner
Ocasional Cortez
Ilhand Omy
Aywanna Pressyou
Rashonme Tobleed

MSNBC-Misleading Spurious News By Cabal
Joyless Reed
Rachel Madcow
Chuck "Tater" Tott
Chris Madviews

CNN-Collusion News Network
Vaina Bash
Jim Acostya
Brian "Alka" Seltzer
Kwis Chromo
Don Leman

Foxy News
Bill Hammer
Martha McCallem
Sean Handitee
Dan Bongoni
Talker Carlson
Maygun Kelly

CBS-Conspiracy Broadcasting System
ABC-Alternative Broadcasting Company
NBC-Newspeak Broadcasting Company
NPR-National Propaganda Radio
ESPN-Entertainment and Sports Program Narcissists

Social Media
Tooter
Mugbook

Newspapers
The Washington Compost
The New York Grimes
The New York Posts

Activist Groups
BLM-*Black Lives Madder*
ANTIFA-*Anti-Freedom Activists*
Proud Guys-*Patriotic Nationalists*
QAnone-*Disinformation Theorists*

Disclaimer:

Any similarity to actual persons or groups, living or dead, or even looking like they're dead, including actual events, is purely coincidental.

This book is a satirical portrayal of fictitious characters and organizations during a mock Presidential campaign/administration and is not intended to be an accurate recreation of any real events or transactions that may have taken place.

Table of Contents

List of Characters 2
Chapter 1-It Never Hurts To Have A Little Insurance 8
Chapter 2-Who's Colluding With The Russians? 29
Chapter 3-Beware of Lame Ducks 41
Chapter 4-Hell To The Thief 60
Chapter 5-Boss! Da Press! Da Press! 82
Chapter 6-It's Muller Time 93
Chapter 7-You're Fired! 111
Chapter 8-Random Acts of Nonsense 124
Chapter 9-The Proof, The Whole Proof, And Nothing
  But the Proof 137
Chapter 10-The Counter Investigation 149
Chapter 11-Impeach, Impeach, Impeach 158
Chapter 12-Does Anyone Know Where The China Virus
  Came From? 168
Chapter 13-The Summer of Our Discontent 179
Chapter 14-Where's Joe? 191
Chapter 15-Lyings and Censors and Snakes...Oh My! 208
Chapter 16-The Final Nail in the Coffin 217

Bela Lugosi

Bela Lugosi was a Hungarian-American actor best remembered for portraying the movie vampire Count Dracula and his roles in many other horror films from 1931 through 1956.

In 1927, he starred as Count Dracula in a Broadway adaptation of Bram Stoker's novel, moving with the play and settling down in Hollywood. He later starred in the 1931 film version of Dracula produced by Universal Pictures. Through the 1930s, he occupied an important niche in horror films. From Bela came the idea of naming a character in the book, Nancy Lugosi.

NOTE:
My thanks to all who have helped me create this book, my wife Shauna, my editor Mark, and most of all God for the inspiration.

Chapter One
It Never Hurts To Have A Little Insurance

The pilot of Trumpet Force One was getting ready to land so he flipped a switch on the flight control panel and said, "Island tower this is India Golf niner niner requesting vectors to the initial, over."

A confused voice on the other end replied, "What?"

The pilot laughed and turned to his co-pilot. "That was a monologue from that animated movie about the super family *The Remarkables*. I've always wanted to say that to a traffic controller." Switching the radio back on, he said, "Yeah, tower, this is Trumpet Force One requesting permission to land, over."

The aircraft controller on the other end replied, "Uh, yeah, Trumpet Force One. You're cleared to land on runway zero zero two. And we're not an island."

"Got it." The pilot turned back to his co-pilot and said, "That guy has no sense of humor."

In the passenger area, Presidential candidate Donald J. Trumpet finished the last bite of a creme sandwich cookie and washed it down with Diet Koke. Trumpet was an intimidating figure, standing 6'3" and weighing just under 240 pounds. His strawberry blonde hair flowed over his head like a breaking wave and his favorite hand gesture was putting his thumb and index fingers together when he was trying to make a point. Dave Bossy, Trumpet's Deputy Campaign Manager, sat in front of him. A stocky figure himself, Bossy had a flat nose and the puffy face of a bulldog with closely cropped, dark hair that was thinning. Bobby Night, the retired college basketball

Chapter 1

coach, sat across from him. Cory Looseandrowsy, Trumpet's Campaign Manager, walked up and down the aisle with a beer in one hand singing, "For he's a jolly good fellow, for he's a jolly good fellow, for he's a jolly good fellowwww..."

"Cory! Sit down!" Trumpet bellowed.

"Which nobody can deny," Looseandrowsy finished, plopping down in one of the seats and immediately falling asleep. He was a thinly built man who looked like a detective and had a bad habit of hitting on stewardesses and female campaign volunteers when he was awake.

"Bobby. What do you think I should start the rally with?" Trumpet asked the retired basketball coach.

Bobby Night rubbed his stubbled chin and said, "If you want to get the crowd excited, throw a few chairs onto the court."

"There won't be a court," Bossy commented.

"In that case, pace back and forth like you want to kill somebody."

"He wants to win voters, not kill them," Bossy explained.

"You don't have to kill them, just look like you want to," Night countered.

"Perhaps I'll save that for when I debate my opponents," Trumpet interjected.

Night shrugged his shoulders and spun a basketball on his index finger. "Can you do that?" he asked Bossy.

Bossy spun a *Make America Terrific Again* hat on his index finger and smirked.

"Dave!" Trumpet shouted. "Quit spinning the merchandise! You'll ruin the shape!"

Bossy quickly put the hat on his head sideways and said, "Sorry, Boss."

"Bill on the front, Dave. Bill on the front. You're not some hip hop artist," Trumpet growled. Then he mumbled, "I should have hired some of the Adventists from my TV reality show."

****

The first Rebubbacan Primary debate was held in Cleveland and sponsored by Foxy News and Mugbook. There were ten male debaters and one female debater, Carly Feeyorina. The moderators were Bret Bear, Chris Wallis, and Maygun Kelly. The moderators took turns firing probing questions at each debater, but it was evident from the very beginning that Kelly didn't like Donald Trumpet... at all.

"Mr. Trumpet," she said with a look resembling a Spanish inquisitor, "you've called women you don't like 'fat pigs,' 'dogs,' 'slobs' and 'disgusting animals.' Does that sound like someone we should elect as President?" Under her breath, she added, "you reprehensible misogynist."

Without batting an eye, although he did bring a baseball bat should the need arise, Trumpet replied, "If a woman is 5'2" and weighs 200 pounds, she's a fat pig. If she pees on the carpet, she's a dog. If she doesn't care how she looks, she's a slob. If she belches in someone's face after eating a garlic pizza, she's a disgusting animal. In fact, if you want to talk disgusting, look at Carly Feeyorina's face. Who would vote for that? Can you imagine *that* face on our next President? I can't even imagine that on a can of dog food."

The crowd booed while the press looked as though someone had just ripped the binky from their mouths. They then went into salivatory mode, knowing they would crucify Trumpet in their reports.

It was not a good debate for him, especially after he

Chapter 1

threatened to fire all the moderators for asking gotcha questions.

His performance in other debates wasn't much better, according to the Washington Compost and New York Grimes. They reported he had the tact of a gorilla, but oddly enough, it was good enough to win the Rebubbacan nomination. The conservatives in America were fed up with Washington politicians and wanted someone in the White House that could get things done. Trumpet had been known in the business world as someone who could do exactly that and he was a Rebubbacan. The conservative public decided to give him a try.

The Autocratic Debates only had five participants and it was essentially a battle between Hillery Clinkton and Bernie Slanders. Slanders was a little too radical for the old school liberals, so Clinkton won the Autocratic nomination pretty much as expected. The stage was set. Orange Godzilla vs. the three-headed monster-Deceptor, Corruptor, and Manipulator.

****

A thin-framed man about 5'10" tall with dark, closely-cropped hair, entered the FBI Director's office in the J. Edgar Hooper building.

"The director is expecting me," the man said to Jim Comby's secretary, who promptly buzzed Comby.

"Director...buzz, buzz...Streter Pzok...buzz...buzz... is here."

"Good, buzz...buzz...send him in," Comby replied.

Streter Pzok entered the spacious office designed in the Art Moderne style. A giant posterized photo of Comby's head hung on the wall behind him bearing an austere look. Other photos of Comby with several Presidents and world leaders (most of them with him photoshopped in) were placed all around the room ending with a display of all of Comby's merit badges he had earned as an eagle scout, his diploma from the College of Bill and Merry, and his Juris Doctor Degree that was the same size as the photo of his head on the wall.

"You wanted to see me, Director?" Pzok asked.

"Yes, Pzok, come in and close the door."

Comby shook his well-groomed head as Pzok approached and said, "For crying out loud, Pzok, zip up your fly."

"I thought it was a little drafty," Pzok stated, taking care of the oversight. "What is it you wanted to see me about, Sir?"

Comby sat back in his soft Corinthian leather chair with a swelling curve, almost falling backwards but righting himself at the last minute. Being 6'8" tall, he looked eye to eye at Pzok when he sat up.

I just wanted to check and see how project 'Dig Up Dirt' on the Big Apple Mafia Social Club was coming along," he replied, with a mouth that was too little for his large face.

"The Big Apple Mafia Social Club?" Pzok repeated with a confused look.

"Trumpet and his cronies," Comby clarified.

"Oh. Well, Sir, so far I've managed to obtain two suits from Trumpet's Dry Cleaners and had them analyzed. Nothing incriminating, just a few ketchup and mustard stains from Burger Emperor. I haven't had a chance to investigate the rest with my dinner parties, kids plays, taking the dog to the vet..."

"Yes, yes, well, keep digging. I'm getting pressure from the Autocrats to get something incriminating on Trumpet and his minions before the Presidential debates."

Chapter 1

"Don't worry, I'll come up with something, Sir."

"You are a good man, Pzok."

"Actually, Sir, the pronoun "you" is now considered offensive. I would rather be referred to as 'your person' or 'Agent Rising Star.'"

"Oh, very well then. *Your person* can refer to me as Director J. Edgar."

"Yes Sir. Was there anything else I can do for you?"

"You said 'you.'"

"You also said 'you.'"

"There, you said it again."

"You did too."

"Enough! Get back to work, Pzok! If you come up with anything, run it by Andy. And bow before you leave."

Pzok stood up and did a quick bow. As he left, he growled and muttered to himself, "He said 'you' again."

****

Leesa Page, a slim FBI attorney with dark brown eyes and hair, laughed when Trumpet was nominated as the Rebubbacan candidate for President. He had about as much chance of beating Hillery as a field mouse in a den of rattlesnakes. She just had to text her clandestine lover, Streter Pzok.

"Well, it looks like the Rebubbacans nominated that misogynistic political amateur that can't stop Tooting. What a joke. He's *not* going to become the President, right? RIGHT?" *Leesa*

Pzok texted her back.

"Stop saying 'right.' You sound like a right wing activist trying to convince someone to join the conservative movement. Of course he's not going to become President. We'll stop it. I have an insurance policy." *Streter*

"What's your insurance got to do with stopping

Trumpet from winning the Presidency?" *Leesa*

"It's not an insurance policy, like for a car, home, or rare stuffed lizard collection, which I have incidentally. It's a plan that should guarantee Trumpet's defeat. I'm gonna run it by Deputy Director McCave. You wanna come with me?" *Streter*

"Yes! YES!" *Leesa*

A hop, skip, and a jump later, they ignored the stares from their fellow bureaucrats at the unusual way they proceeded down the hall, and entered Andy McCave's grotto-like office. Mining lights hung across the ceiling and a few fruit bats dangled by their feet from the electrical cords. It was a room Nancy Lugosi would have felt very

Chapter 1

comfortable in.

"Close the door," the Deputy Director with short graying hair, dark eyes and dark eyebrows uttered.

Page shut the door then she and Pzok entered.

"Excuse the mess, I'm remodeling," McCave said as they sat down.

"You asked for this meeting, so what's on your mind, Pzok?" McCave asked.

Pzok sat up straight in his chair, cracked his knuckles, and grinned like a young mountain lad who just had his first taste of moonshine... before he threw up.

"I have a plan to keep Trumpet from becoming our next President," Pzok confidently stated, giving Leesa a tight-lipped smile.

She gave him a loving look and coyly twirled a strand of hair around her finger.

"What's your plan?" McCave asked.

"Trumpet has a campaign volunteer named Carder Page..."

"No relation!" Leesa quickly remarked, putting up both hands and waving them side to side.

McCave gave her a suspicious look and made a mental note to look into her genealogy.

"Anyway," Pzok continued, "he worked in Moscow for three years as a broker for Merril Linch. I'll accuse him of being a Russian spy and say he's Trumpet's contact with the Kremlin. If he's a spy, then Trumpet is a spy. Voila! What red-blooded patriot would elect a Russian spy? And if that doesn't work, I'll accuse his other campaign staffers of being Russian spies too. Whadya think?"

McCave sat back and looked up at the bats in the ceiling. Like a forest cat, he lurched forward and pulled out a Glock from his top drawer fixed with a silencer. "Pop!

Pop! Pop!" he fired, hitting every one of the squeaking creatures and leaving nothing but splattered bat guts on the ceiling and floor. "I hate those flying rats," he snarled.

"That was some fine shooting," Page commented.

McCave blew the smoke from the muzzle. With a thin-lipped smile, he said, "If you think that was good, you should see me with my M82."

"So, what do you think of my plan?" Pzok asked, like a schoolboy waiting for his teacher to give him the expected "A."

McCave rubbed his square chin to create suspense, then pursed his lips like a Louis Fuitton handbag and said, "I'll run it by the Director. Good work, Pzok."

Pzok proudly threw out his chest.

Not to be outdone, Page threw hers out too, popping a button on her blouse which flipped up and hit Mc-Cave's forehead.

"It's a good thing that wasn't a bullet," McCave remarked, "or I'd be a dead man."

"Sorry, Andy," Page apologized.

"That's Deputy Director McCave," he corrected her.

"Yes, I meant Deputy Director," Page stated, with her dull, brown eyes avoiding his critical gaze.

As the two left McCave's grotto, Page said, "McCave sure acted grouchy. He must be constipated again."

"He's always constipated," Pzok stated. "The man never eats enough roughage."

They walked a little farther, then Page said, "I want to believe the plan you outlined for Andy is going to work and there's no way Trumpet gets elected. We just can't take the risk of that narcissistic ninny becoming president."

Pzok gave her a smug smile and said, "My plan will

insure he won't see the interior of the White House, if he doesn't die before the election. Accidentally, of course."

"Ooo, I love it when you talk sinister," Page cooed.

****

Pzok's next move was to go after one of Trumpet's campaign volunteers, George Papacropolis. He was a short Greek-American with dark features that could have passed for a kid in grade school if he didn't have a five o'clock shadow.

A week later, Papacropolis was at an upmarket bar called The Queen's English Tavern in London sharing a few drinks with an Australian diplomat named Alex Downunder. He happened to mention something about Russians having Hillery's emails in normal conversation. It went like this:

"Oy, mate," Downunder greeted Papacropolis. "Yer on Trumpet's campaign staff aren't you?"

"It depends," Papacropolis, wearing large black-rimmed sunglasses, answered cautiously. "If you like Trumpet, then yes. If you don't, then no."

Downunder chuckled like a woodchuck in a lumber mill, then said, "Goodun, Mate. But hey, I heard on the news that the Russkis might have some of Hillery's emails. You know anything about that?"

"It's true. I even saw a few of them," Papacropolis replied proudly, rubbing his prickly chin. He then leaned close to his Aussie friend and said, "They not only contained emails about the Clinkton's shady business dealings, but classified government stuff, and all the private recipes from the TV show, Hades Kitchen too."

"No way, Mate. Why, the Russians could create entire seven course dinners with those recipes!"

"All they would have to do is order the ingredients

from Amazone, kidnap a few master chefs, and they'd surpass the free world in the culinary arts. No more bread lines in Stalingrad!" Papacropolis stated, like the world was on the verge of collapse.

"It's called Volvograd now," Downunder corrected him. "So who you gonna call?"

"Well it ain't Spookbusters," Papacropolis said, causing both men to laugh uncontrollably. Unfortunately, his words would get the twenty-nine-year-old into trouble down the road, like a retreaded tire with 100,000 miles on it.

****

Hillery sat behind her desk in the *Clinkton For President* campaign headquarters with a glass of Domane Leroy Musigny Grand Crew in her hand. Looking at the label, she said, "I really like this Domane Leroy Musigee... Musighnee... I need a wine with a name that's easier to pronounce. She turned to her campaign manager, Robby Muuk, who looked like a conservative college professor with short, wiry hair and glasses, and said, "Have you seen those crass red baseball caps Trumpet is giving to his supporters that say *Make America Terrific Again*?"

"Yes I have," Muuk said, with his unusual wide, squinty smile. "I think we should have blue hats printed with the slogan, *Make Hillery Terrific Again*."

"I'm already terrific, you nitwit," she said, putting the glass up to her thin, red lips and taking a sip. "Besides, my supporters would think we're copying Trumpet's idea."

"You mean all the bureaucrats in Washington. D.C."

"Yes, and everyone else in D.C. too," she stated, turning her sloped nose up like a turnip.

"According to the Poles, you also have 48 of the

Chapter 1

50 states... but the Hungarians say you have 49," Muuk added, flipping the name tag connected to the lanyard around his neck.

Clinkton sprang from her chair, spilling her drink on her Debbie Wiggam high heeled shoes, and shouted, "Which lousy state *doesn't* support me?"

"Utah," Muuk replied meekly, cowering behind a sixteen year-old female campaign volunteer.

"Damn pious Mormons," she grumbled. "We need to guarantee that all 50 states will vote for me. I want to destroy Trumpet completely. What do you suggest?"

"How about...we say Trumpet made a deal with the Russians to help him win the election," Muuk said, pointing toward the ceiling with his index finger.

"Hmmm," Clinkton mused. "That's good, but I think I need a few other brains to figure the details on just *how* he conspired with the Russians."

"You want me to visit the morgue?" Muuk offered, wringing his hands.

"Hail no!" Clinkton replied, with her best Arkansas accent. "Call Mark Elieus, he has a brilliant mind."

"You want me to remove his brain?" Muuk asked.

Clinkton let out an exasperated sigh and said, "Nevermind, I'll call him."

"Mark Elieus," the voice on the phone said.

"Mark, this is Hillery."

"Hillery who?"

"Clinkton!"

"Oh, that Hillery. Hi Hill. What can I do you in for?"

"I really need your help, Mark. Can you drop what you're doing and help me frame Trumpet so I'm the next President?"

"Well, Hill, my law firm is pretty busy right now. I

could do it, but it would be expensive."

"How expensive?"

"Just send me a check for one million dollars and I'll get the ball rolling."

"What are you going to do? Build a bowling alley?"

"Hey, it costs money to frame people properly, Hill. You need a really nice gold frame with museum glass, diamond inlays, cotton mat boards..."

"I want him destroyed, not a picture of him!" she bellowed.

"Oh, you said 'Frame.'"

"THEN I SAID 'DESTROY!'"

"Okay but that will cost $12.4 million."

She muttered an undiscernible curse word then said, "I'll have to see if I can get the Autocratic National Committee to go in on the costs as well."

"Great! As soon as the check arrives I'll get right on it," he promised, hanging up the phone. He sat back in his leather chair with a grin that would have put The Joker to shame. Then he realized the project was too big for him to handle alone. He needed people who would go dumpster diving and swim in cesspools to find the dirt on someone. He thought for a moment, then nodded like a bobblehead doll and said, "Fusion Gyps."

****

After setting up a meeting with Glen Simpleton, the head honcho at Fusion Gyps, the bald and bespectacled Mark Elieus arrived at Simpleton's office to start planning their opposition research on the most evil man since Boris Badenuf (villain on the Rocky and Bullwrinkle show). In other words...♪dum dum dum dum♪... Donald Trumpet.

Pulling out a folder from his briefcase that had a list of Trumpet's friends and associates since kindergarten, Elieus

Chapter 1

said, "Here's a record I compiled of everyone who came into contact with Trumpet since he was a kindygartner."

"Looks more like a folder to me," Simpleton stated.

"A written record," Elieus stated slowly.

"Oh," Simpleton responded.

Elieus took in a deep breath and asked, "Any ideas off the top of your head on what angle should we take to make him look bad so Clinkton gets the presidency?"

The curly gray-haired Simpleton put his hands up to form a triangle and replied, "A 45 degree might work."

Elieus shook his head. "No, I meant what plan should we devise to make Trumpet look like a fool?"

"Well, we could steal all his suits and replace them with court jesters' outfits."

Elieus gritted his teeth and said, "I need something that will get the public to really hate him so they vote for her."

Simpleton gazed upward and replied, "You ever notice how many moving tiles there are in my ceiling?"

"No, Glen, I haven't. Concentrate on the problem, will you?"

"I think I'll need to put on my thinking cap for this one." Simpleton turned around and picked up a 1992 Washington Redskins Super Bowl Champions baseball hat that sat on a souvenir shelf behind him. Putting it firmly on his head, he grimaced then said, "How about... we say he started hiring bourgeoisie on his TV show to discriminate against the proletariat?"

"STOP WITH THE MARXIST RHETORIC AND COME UP WITH A PRACTICAL SOLUTION!" Elieus roared, causing Simpleton's hat to crinkle up and disintegrate from Elieus' caustic breath.

Simpleton reached up and brushed off the cotton residue from his hair and, with a look that matched his crushed hat, muttered, "You disintegrated my Redskins Super Bowl Champions baseball cap."

Elieus tossed the lukewarm Cappuccino in his face he had brought with him from Spendbucks and growled, "Snap out of it, Glen!"

A sudden look of confusion came over Simpleton's face. He looked around and said, "Where am I?"

"You're at Fusion Gyps and we're trying to come up with a scheme to prevent Donald Trumpet from winning the presidency," Elieus stated, as though he was talking to his pet dog.

"Oh, right. For a moment I thought I was in an episode of "Man From My UNCLE and I was that Russian spy, Illya Cureyakin being waterboarded. I'm okay now."

"You're sure you're okay?" Elieus asked with one raised eyebrow.

"Yes, I just need to cut back on the psilocybin mushrooms I put in my salad." He then pursed his lips, looking like he was going to kiss a fish and said, "Okay, destroy Trumpet... destroy Trumpet." A dim bulb suddenly appeared above his head as he exclaimed, "I've got it! How about we say since he's an international businessman, he made a deal with Pootin to let him build hotels in Russia and share the revenue with him if Russia would help him win the election?"

"Hmmm," Elieus thought, as he assumed the pose of August Rodin's sculpture *The Thinker*. "You might have something there. I'll advance you a million bucks to get started."

"A million and thirty-five," Simpleton countered.

Chapter 1

"What's the thirty-five for?" Elieus asked.

"My Redskins thinking cap you destroyed," Simpleton replied.

"I could have bought that on Amazone for 25 bucks," Elieus grumbled. "All right... deal."

They shook hands and did the Hokey Pokey then Elieus left.

Simpleton's first move was to pick his nose, then his team. The name Nellie Odohr popped into his head like a pop tart. She had a degree in Russian literature, was an expert in cybersecurity, and was fluent in Russian, Farsi, and Klingon. The best part was that she worked there.

"Griselda," Simpleton called out to his secretary, "call Nellie Odohr on the 6th floor and tell her to come to my office."

"Right away, Mr. Elieus," his secretary snorted.

A moment later, a plain- looking, fifty-four-year-old woman with collar-length grayish brown hair and glasses appeared, smelling of cigarettes and an overabundance of *Black Scat* perfume.

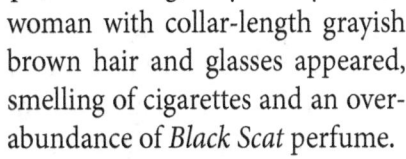

The first thing he said when she walked in the room was, "What's the suitcase for?"

"It's a handbag," she corrected him. "It's mostly for a very expensive line of cosmetics I carry with me so I can freshen up when I need to."

He was about to suggest she should "freshen up," but he didn't want to start off on the wrong foot, since he was right-footed.

Instead he smiled chillingly and said, "I have a project I want you to help me with. Come in and sit down."

"What is it? she asked, taking a seat across from him. The scent of her perfume hit him like a garbage truck.

He waved away the miasma that swirled around his head and pointed to a chair across the room. "Would you mind taking a seat over there?"

"Sure," she acquiesced, reminding herself not to use a half bottle of perfume next time she got ready for work.

When she was far enough away to stop his eyes from watering, he said, "I called you in because I've been hired to put together a team to destroy Donald Trumpet so Clinkton is elected President and I want you to be on it."

"I'd love to," she beamed. "My husband and I were big donors to her campaign, you know."

"Yes, that's why I thought you would be perfect. You play favorites for the right team. I'm thinking of accusing Trumpet of colluding with the Russians to affect the outcome of the election, something along those lines. We just need some incriminating material to back it up."

"You know, Christopher Steel would be someone to consider putting on the team. He has contacts in Russia you might be able to use."

"I don't wear contacts," Simpleton stated, shaking his head.

"I meant he has people there he can contact," Odohr clarified.

"Oh. Good idea. Let's go to Steel's office and recruit him for the project." Simpleton stood up and swatted an imaginary fly away from his head.

Simpleton and Odohr took the elevator to the second floor then walked down a long hall lined with glass office doors until they came to a steel office door with a

Chapter 1

bolted nameplate that said "Chris-Man of Steel."

After knocking on the door, Simpleton rubbed his knuckles and said, "Ow!"

"Wimp," she muttered, pretending to cough.

From the other side of the door, a muted voice asked, "What's the password?"

Simpleton and Odohr looked at each other and shrugged their shoulders.

"I don't *have* a password, Steel," Simpleton boomed. "This is your boss. Open the door or I'll have security break it down."

The door slowly opened making an eerie creaking sound. A small-framed man with slightly graying hair and squinty eyes cautiously peered out and said, "Close enough. Come in to my lair. And who's this? Has she been vetted?" he asked, pointing both index fingers at Odohr.

"Nellie Odohr," Simpleton replied. "She works on the sixth floor."

"Oh, right, I don't get up to the sixth floor much," Steel remarked. "In fact, I don't get out of my office much." Suddenly putting his hands over his ears, he rocked from side to side, crying, "Because of the bells! The bells!"

Simpleton and Odohr looked at him like he was having a baby.

"That was my *Hunchback of Noter Dame* impersonation," he informed them proudly. "I'm a master of impersonations, you know."

"Yes, well, Nellie here is going to be assisting me with a project and I want you to help," Simpleton stated.

Steel hopped around the room and clapped his hands saying, "Oh goody goody gumdrops. ♪A project, a project."♪

"How old *are* you?" Odohr asked, casting a wary

25

look at him she would give a patient in a psych ward.

He leaned close to her and replied, "I was just showing you that I can disguise myself to fit any character. That was my Susan Olson."

She gave him a puzzled look.

"You know... Cindy on the Bratty Bunch!" he exclaimed.

She moved a short distance away and glanced around his office. "You've got quite a collection of James Bomd posters... and is that an Astin Marton?" she asked, pointing at a miniature version of the car facing her, next to the back wall of the office."

"Yes, it is," he stated proudly. "It's a kit I built myself. I use it as my desk." He pointed to two chairs in front of the car/desk and said, "Have a seat."

After Simpleton and Odohr sat down, Steel jumped in the driver's seat. "I had the roof removed so I could get in and out easily. The passenger ejection seat actually works. You wanna see?"

"No, that's okay," Simpleton remarked,

Steel smiled and asked, "So what's the capon?"

"That's 'caper,'" Odohr corrected him,

"Yeah, yeah, what's the caper?"

Simpleton sat back in his chair and said, "We're gonna destroy Trumpet so Clinkton wins the election."

Steel leaned forward with a sparkle in his eyes and said, "I know a Russian assassin that works cheap."

"No, I don't want to kill him, just show that he colluded with the Russians to win the election."

"We need a dossier," Odohr replied. "Something that ties him in with the Kremlin and the upcoming election."

Steel wrung his hands together and chuckled, "Heh, heh, heh. Child's play. I used to do this kind of stuff for

Chapter 1

Mission Impossible Six in London all the time. When do you want it?"

"The sooner the better," Simpleton replied.

Steel gave them a smug smile and said, "I'll make a few calls to some people I know and should have something for you in a month or two."

"We don't have much time, this has to be done before the election. The whole project is being funded by Hillery Clinkton, so money is no object," Simpleton stated.

Steel began to drool at the thought of an unlimited expense account, then wiped it off his mouth and said, "That was my dog impersonation."

Odohr gave Steel a look of disgust as Simpleton said, "You might start with a rumor I was told that Trumpet was caught in a video with some young hookers at the Moscow Ritzy Carlton Hotel in 2013."

"Sounds like a promising lead," Steel stated, through narrowed Jason Born eyes.

"Good!" Simpleton and Odohr stood up to leave.

Steel sprang out of his chair and shook Simpleton's hand then gave Odohr a business card that said *"World's Greatest Secret Agent; Espionage, Counter Espionage, Man of a Thousand Identities; For Free Estimates Call (007) 007-0007."* She took the card and put it in a portable paper shredder she had in her handbag.

"What's that buzzing sound?" Steel asked.

"Must be the alarm clock I keep in my purse," Odohr replied.

"Oh. Well, when I come up with something I'll give you one ringy dingy," he assured them.

When Simpleton and Odohr stood there with blank stares, he said, "That was my Lily Tumlin... you know, Ernestine the telephone operator skit on Laugh Out? I watch all the re-runs on Primetime Video."

Simpleton and Odohr rolled their eyes, shook their heads and quickly left.

Steel walked back to his desk, took out his Walthor PPK airsoft pistol from the jockey box then whirled around and fired a dart at the James Bomd poster *To Russia With Love*. The dart struck James Bomd's blonde arch-enemy from the movie, between the eyes. Steel then blew the imaginary smoke from the barrel and said, "Yes, I've still got it."

Chapter Two
Who's Colluding With The Russians?

Steel held the button down on his cell phone and said, "Sirie... call the Ritzy Carlton in Moscow."

"Calling a Moscow store for Ritzy crackers," Sirie verified.

"No! No! The Ritzy Carlton Hotel," Steel yawped.

"Calling a hotel that has Ritzy Crackers," Sirie said.

"NO! THE RITZY CARLTON HOTEL IN MOSCOW!" Steel yelled.

"Could you repeat that," Sirie asked.

"Nyah," Steel cried, whacking the phone on his desk a few times. With clenched teeth, he looked up the number in an old Moscow phone directory he had and dialed it himself. "Stupid Sirie," he mumbled as the line rang.

"Moskva Ritzy Carlton," a voice answered on the other end.

"Yes, I'd like to speak to the Head Clerk there and I'm not talking about the clerk in charge of the bathrooms," Steel stated.

"Ah, an American. This is head desk clerk, what can I do you for?"

"Yes, my name is Dave Bossy and I'm Donald Trumpet's campaign manager," Steel lied. "I understand there was a video made in 2013 at your hotel that could be embarrassing to him. It was where he was with some young girls. Do you have any copies?"

"Of de girls?" the clerk asked.

"Yes, the girls in the video with Mister Trumpet."

"Da," the clerk replied, "Mister Trumpet vas given copies of dat video."

"Unfortunately, Mister Trumpet lost them. Can you

describe what is on the video to make sure it is the one I'm referring to?" Steel asked.

"Of course. It vas music video of Miss Unifarce pageant here at hotel. Mr. Trumpet's singink vas, you could say, embarrassing."

"Uh, it wasn't pornographic?" Steel asked.

The clerk laughed. "Of course not. But if you vant embarrassing videos of Trumpet ve have surveillance of him pooping in his bathroom."

"No, that's all right," Steel responded. "Thanks for your help."

"Of course, Mr. Bossy. Alvays happy to help our friends across de vater. By the vay, your voice has definite British accent."

"Yes, I was born in England but I came to the U.S. on a student visa and just overstayed. Thanks again." Steel hung up and sighed. He had to make more phone calls to Russia. He would have gone there personally, but Pootin's Foreign Unintelligence Service had a "Shoot to Kill" order on him because of the espionage work he did in Russia as a British spy. He had turned several Russian diplomats who defected and also stole Pootin's favorite horse he liked to ride with his shirt off.

It was as clear as a window that had just been washed with the Russian window cleaner called "Vindex" that he wasn't going to get any usable intel from Russia. Then he remembered there were some expatriated Russians living in London. He would go there and interview them. He had Glen Simpleton authorize the Fusion Gyps private jet to make the trip and he was soon off to the land of tea and crummy pets.

Upon landing at Heathenrow Airport, he went to Baggage Claim and picked up his suitcase and pet carrier

Chapter 2

containing his Chinese long-haired cat he named Meow Tse Tung. Once he arrived in his "safe" flat, he went right to work. After putting his bullet-proof suits in the closet, he unpacked his suitcase then made a call to an ex-Russian official named Igor Sikorsky, who had changed his name to Ivan Awfulitch. Sikorsky was one of the officials Steel spirited out of Russia and consequently owed him a favor.

After dialing the number for Ivan Awfulitch, Steel sat back in his bunny slippers that had retractable daggers on the tips and custom robe that had "World's Greatest Secret Agent" embroidered on the back.

"Hallo?" Awfulitch answered.

"Ivan!" Steel exclaimed.

"Who is this?" Sikorsky asked.

"It's your old pal, Chris Steel."

"Comrade Chris, I thought the Russians had liquidated you," Sikorsky/Awfulitch bellowed.

"Nope, I'm still alive and kicking," Steel replied.

"You still have those dagger-tipped slippers you purchased from Spies-R-Us?" Sikorsky asked.

"Yep, I still have them. Hey, Igor, I mean Ivan, I need a favor."

"What is favor, my friend?"

"I need you to write out a deposition saying you have information that Trumpet had clandestine meetings with Russian officials, spies, and prostitutes. I'll embellish it a little when you're done."

"What do I get for dis?"

"One hundred pounds of Klopse and one hundred bottles of vodka. I'll give you half now and the other half after you provide what I want," Steel replied.

"Make it two hundred each and I'll do it."

"You drive a hard bargain, but since we're old

friends, I'll see what I can do."

"Last time you said dat, I vas hanggliding into Estonia instead of being transported by British helicopter."

Steel began to laugh that ended in a coughing spasm. When he had regained his composure, he said, "Yes, I feel bad about that, Ivan, but we got you out, didn't we?"

"Da, I'm just glad dat Russia didn't send any Migs after me vhen I made escape."

Steel chuckled. "Even if they had sent Migs, the poorly trained pilots would have probably thought you were a kite. Stay close to your phone, I'll be in touch."

"Next time I see you, ve drink to old times, da? You bring Vodka."

"Will do." Steel hung up the phone and made himself a martini... shaken not stirred, then picked up Meow and sat down in his plush easy chair. Holding his drink in one hand, he stroked his cat with the other until the feline emitted an evil purr. His plan was coming together.

****

A week later, Steel delivered the promised goods to Sikorsky/Awfulitch and obtained the narrative he requested. He converted the info into a dossier (adding his own embellishments), then sent the documents by way of special courier to Glen Simpleton at Fusion Gyps.

When the packet arrived with Steel's return address, Simpleton ripped open the envelope with all the enthusiasm of a child opening his first present on Christmas morning. With eyes the size of golf balls, he began to read all the sordid details of secret meetings, kinky sex, and hush money paid. It was better than he had imagined and was sure to keep the bellicose businessman out of the White House. He had to let Hillery Clinkton know he had the goods on Trumpet that would assure her nomination

Chapter 2

as the next President of the United States.

"Hello, Hillery? Glen Simpleton here. Have I got a surprise for you!"

"Ooooh, what is it, Glen?" she replied, chomping at the Bit-of-Honey candy she had in her mouth.

"I shouldn't say anything over the phone in case someone is listening. Why don't you meet me here at Fusion Gyps and I'll show you."

"I'll be right over as soon as I finish breaking the last of my government mobile phones with a hammer."

"Great! See you then."

"Not if I see you first," Clinkton said with a chuckle, hanging up the phone.

That afternoon she arrived at Fusion Gyps and went directly to Glen Simpleton's office.

"Hillery Clinkton is here," Simpleton heard on his phone intercom from his secretary.

"Send her in," Simpleton instructed.

The door opened and Robby Muuk stood aside and announced, "Mr. Simpleton. The next President of the United States!" He then bowed and Hillery Clinkton glided in wearing a shawl made of real Striped Skunk fur, earrings made from Treecreeper beaks, and a necklace made from Pocket Gopher teeth.

With her double chin in the air, she strolled over to Simpleton who gave her a kiss on her puffy cheek. She then sat down across from him and said, "So, what is this big surprise, Glen?"

"First may I say your perfume is divine, Hillery."

Clinkton smiled with a look of haughty disdain and said, "Thank you, Glen. It's called "Eau de Ruby Throated Hummingbird Sap."

"It's certainly more pleasant than that paint remover

that Nellie Odohr wears, but don't tell her I said that."

"Don't worry, Glen. Your secret is safe with me." Turning to Muuk standing by the door, she said, "Rob, make a note of that."

Muuk quickly scribbled on the palm of his hand with a Sharpey.

"Your jewelry is also quite, a, unique," Simpleton added.

"Yes, it's called Arkansas Chic. So, don't keep me in suspense, Glen. Where is my big surprise?"

Simpleton chuckled like an IRS agent about to tell a citizen they were going to be audited and replied, "I have a dossier put together by one of my top men that makes Trumpet look like a depraved lecherous sex fiend worse than that guy back in the late 90's who was President."

"That was my husband," Clinkton reminded him.

"Oh, yes, that's right. Actually, I meant the guy back in the early 40's who was the Führer in Germany," Simpleton stated with a wide smile.

Clinkton gave him a cold look, as miniature icicles formed on her eyelashes, and said, "Just show me the surprise, Glen."

Simpleton handed her the dossier and sat back with a hopeful look on his face.

Clinkton put on her horn-rimmed glasses made from gold-plated elk antlers and began to read. Her expression began with a nefarious smile that eventually turned into a concerned frown.

Simpleton noticed her apparent look of concern and asked, "Is anything wrong, Hillery?"

"No, this is good work, but it seems too good. And I'm wondering if we really need it. According to the Poles and the Hungarians, Trumpet has about as much a chance

Chapter 2

of winning the presidency as Joe Hiden has becoming President in the future."

Simpleton put up his hands and said, "Now, let's not be hasty, Hill. I still think this can guarantee a victory for you. I'll contact my man in London and have him share this with his intelligence contacts and let this information leak to the press. I'm telling you, Hillery, don't take this guy Trumpet too lightly or he's liable to sell you an ice skating rink."

Clinkton mulled it over for a moment then said, "All right, Glen. we'll use it as a last resort. How much do you need to continue?"

"Oh, a quarter million will do for now," Simpleton replied, rubbing his hands together.

"Rob. Write Glen a check," Clinkton ordered.

Muuk whipped out a check book and filled out the agreed amount. He then took it over for Clinkton to sign. After putting her John Hancock on the check, she handed it to Simpleton.

"This signature says "*John Hancock*," Simpleton remarked, handing the check back to her.

"Oh, I must have been thinking Presidentially. Rob, give me another check," Clinkton ordered.

Muuk quickly filled out another one.

"There you go," Clinkton said, handing him another check with the correct signature.

"Thank you, Hillery. I'll contact my man and we'll get the ball rolling."

Clinkton stood up and said, "What is it with you men and bowling alleys?"

"It's... never mind. I'll get right on it."

"Excellent," Hillery stated.

****

Things were looking up for Hillery Clinkton. The only concern she had was the FBI investigation into the private server she had been using instead of a government server that had thousands of official state department emails on it. *"Oh, not to worry, I wiped the server with Vindex. Ha, ha,"* she was quoted in the New York Grimes as saying.

Her personal email server was first discovered in 2012, by a House committee investigating the attack on the Consulate in Bengahzi. The FBI conducted a lengthy investigation lasting four years and just before the election, Director Comby stated that although her use of a private server was extremely careless, thoughtless, diabolical, underhanded, and probably put countless lives in danger, the FBI would not press charges. But Hillery wasn't out of the woods yet. She still had some thick foliage to get through. An investigation was launched by the FBI involving child pornography that happened to be on her aide's personal computer at home. The pornographic images belonged to her aide's husband, Tony Wiener (an appropriate name) but 600,000 new government emails were discovered. A new investigation was launched like one of the early German V2 rockets and given to Andy McCave.

Pzok walked into McCave's grotto and said, "You wanted to see me, Andy?"

"That's Deputy Director, Pzok." McCave quickly raised his Glock and fired. "Pop!"

"What the...!" Pzok uttered, noticing the bullet had grazed his shoulder near his lapel.

McCave blew the smoke from his pistol and said, "There was a spider on your jacket but I took care of it. Now the reason I called you in is because I just found out that more of Hillery's emails were discovered on one of

Chapter 2

Hooma Abedine's private computers at home belonging to her husband. We have to reopen the investigation."

"Are you serious?" Pzok asked, looking at the mark where the bullet grazed him from the spider execution.

"Yes, and be thorough." (wink, wink)

"Do you have something in your eye?" Pzok asked.

"No... take all the time you need!" (wink, wink)

"There's definitely something in your eye," Pzok pressed.

"I expect a report tomorrow, now get out of my office!" McCave shouted.

"Ohh," Pzok exclaimed. (wink, wink)

Dashing out of McCave's cave, he hurried back to his desk and sat down. He had to text Leesa and let her know Hillery was being investigated again.

"Hey Hottie Body, I just got assigned to investigate a new bunch of Hillery emails on Abedine's computer." *Streter*

"You aren't going to do it, are you? This could hurt her chances of becoming President." *Leesa*

"Don't worry, this isn't a ticking terrorist bomb," he typed.

At that moment, his watch alarm went off making him jump and have a minor wet accident in his trousers.

"Streter? You still there?" Leesa texted.

Running to the bathroom with a clean pair of briefs (he had extras in his desk drawers), Pzok cursed and threw his watch in the toilet just in case it was a plant and had an explosive device attached.

****

The next day, Pzok walked into McCave's office and handed him a folder that said, "Midyear Examination."

"What's this, Pzok. Your grades from high school?"

"No," Pzok replied. "That's the code name I gave the investigation into Hillery's additional emails."

"Oh." McCave browsed through the report and said, "So, all you found were recipes and dirty jokes?"

"Yeah," Pzok replied, showing his best lecherous expression. "She had some doozies. Of course, I deleted all the rest that were incriminating."

"Good work. I'll let Comby know the investigation is complete and we can put this email thing to rest along with the other investigations we ran on the Clinktons and put in the circular file. Now all we have to do is wait for Hillery to crush that narcissistic Cro Magnon in the election and send him back to his New York outhouse."

"The debates should be fun. I can't wait to watch them with my lov... er, wife," Pzok stated, as beads of guilty sweat formed on his forehead like a car window treated with Rainex water repellent.

****

By November Hillery had picked out the decor, carpets, and drapes for the oval office. The Uranium scandal where she allowed Russians to buy all the uranium in the country, during her time as Secretary of State, was in her rear view mirror, thanks to Adam Shifty's investigation. He said it was an orchestrated distraction by the Rebubbacan Symphony Orchestra and dismissed it, even though the Russians had deposited over two million dollars in the Clinkton's Family Foundation. Shifty also came through for her in the Bengawzi investigation, saying the deaths of the personnel that occurred in the embassy because of the deadly attack were tragic but military support couldn't have reached them in time anyway. Clinkton's delaying the embassy's request to send help for several hours had nothing to do with it. And thanks to the FBI, the email server

Chapter 2

brouhaha was conveniently dismissed, even though Comby did say a few uncomplimentary things about her. Yes, the debates would be just a formality and then she would become the first female President of the **universe**! Well, that would be the next step.

****

The day finally arrived for the Presidential debates and Hillery was as confident as a boa constrictor with a ring tailed lemur in its coils. The debates went back and forth, tooth and nail, keeping dentists and manicurists busy until it was time to vote for America's President. Clinkton had all the major news outlets supporting her besides the major social media outlets, so she felt as smug as a college girl with all the test answers written on the palm of her hand. In fact, she had all the answers to the debate questions written on the back of her hand ahead of time. Trumpet would need a miracle whip.

But... even though all the hostile news outlets had already written his political epitaph, Trumpet rose from the ashes like the Phoenix bird from Arizona. Not only did he get a miracle whip, he got the whole sandwich. When all the votes were cast and the electoral college finally tallied up its numbers, Trumpet had won the presidency and Hillery was stuck with the bill for all the interior decorations she had purchased for the White House.

The announcement to the public that Trumpet won had Clinkton supporters screaming in agony and Trumpet supporters cheering and waving American flags. Half the country that supported Hillery threatened they would move to Mexico, until they learned that Mexico wouldn't allow immigrants. The other half that supported Trumpet held victory rallies and kept baseball cap manufacturers and flag companies working overtime.

Trumpet Toot: I won the electoral college by a landslide! Hillery claims to have won the popular vote but dead people don't count.

Chapter Three
Beware of Lame Ducks

Hillery slouched in her desk chair with sandbags under her eyes from being up all night. Clumps of her dyed blonde hair littered the floor. She held a half full bottle of Arkansas bourbon whiskey in one hand, and a copy of the New York Grimes in the other that said, "FBI trying to link Trumpet to Russians." An email on her laptop read "You're fired! Warmest Regards, Donald." Posters lining the walls of her main campaign headquarters had the slogan, "What the Hell...Vote for Hill!" and hundreds of balloon animals still remained in a large net above her that were supposed to be released for her victory celebration. Now they would have to wait until New Years. An unopened case of Tequila from the Mexican President sat in the break room and a box of Cuban victory cigars sat by the door that unfortunately she would have to smoke by herself. A photo of Vladamir Pootin stared at her from a table nearby that said, "Hillery, thanks a million for the uranium, in fact thanks a couple of million."

Still numb from the results, she couldn't believe that a private sector cretin had won the Presidential Election from a seasoned political apparatchik such as herself. Through clenched teeth she muttered, "How could this imbecile have a majority of the electoral votes when I won the popular vote? He *must* have cheated more than I did." Now her dream of being The President was ruined but she could still destroy the man who took her rightful throne. She needed Buhrock Obahma's help. He was a lame duck, but he could still quack pretty loud so she decided to give him a call.

"Hello, Buhrock? Hillery here."

"Hillery! Hey, I've been meaning to (burp) call you but I've been busy with the transition, you know."

"That's what I'm calling about, Buhrock. You know all those funny Mugbook ads Russian hackers posted about me on the internet?"

"Yeah, what about them?"

"We can say that the Russians interfered in our election to get Trumpet elected and he coordinated the whole thing! Then we impeach him."

"How are you going to (burp) prove that? Sorry, I

Chapter 3

just ate a taco."

"Speaking of tacos, I have a team that has some spicy stuff on Trumpet that shows that he's chummy with the Russians. We get Congress to assign an investigator to look into it and staff the investigatory body with liberal lawyers. Congress impeaches him and he's out."

Obahma wiped the taco sauce off his mouth and said, "I like it. I can also have my press secretary make an announcement in the White House briefing room that Trumpet knew the Russians hacked the election and helped them."

"Would you do that for me?" Hillery gushed.

"Sure. A Rebubbacan may be President, but the Autocratic Party owns the bureaucrats. We'll have Trumpet out on his ear before his first year is over."

Hillery went into a fit of demonic laughter and kissed her picture of Pootin.

The next day, Obahma's White House Press Secretary, Josh Disearnest, stood at the briefing podium and told all the reporters to take their seats.

After they obliged, Disearnest said, "Uh, if you would kindly bring back those chairs I'll get started with the briefing, if you don't mind."

The reporters looked at him with confused stares, then shrugged their shoulders, put the chairs back, and sat down.

Disearnest cleared his throat and began. "First of all, it is a fact and I have it on tape..." he reached in his Pzoket and pulled out a cassette tape that read, "Alvin and the Churchmonk's Greatest Hits." Holding it up for all to see, and making sure that no one could read the label, he gasped as it slipped from his hand and fell on the floor, cracking open and spilling the polyester plastic film all over. Picking it up in ribbons, he gave an embarrassed smile and said, "Don't worry, we have back-ups." He then continued with his announcement. "The Rebubbacan nominee for President, Donald Trumpet, did in fact collude with Russia to provide disinformation on his opponent, Hillery Clinkton, besides hacking into our election database in order to help win the Presidency."

Reporters in the room gave a collective gasp and one man fainted. He was a White House tour guide that sneaked in and passed out because his blood sugar level was down.

****

The Autocrats immediately went on the attack. Diane Finestine and Adam Shifty appeared together on CNN during a Vaina Bash interview.

Bash: "I have Senator Finestine and Congressman Shifty with me who claim the election was a result of cheating by Donald Trumpet who worked closely with the Russians to win the election. Senator Finestine, could you elaborate for our viewers?"

Finestine: "Yes, I can Vaina. And may I say your hair is divine. Who does it?"

Bash: "Why, thank you Senator. I go to Patrick Seguy Hair Salon on 15th. I also have my manicures and pedicures done there as well."

Finestine: "Well, it looks very stunning."

Bash: "Yes, I know. So, how do you think Trumpet cheated?"

Finestine: "He had to cheat. Nobody could have beaten Hillery in a fair election. Not even God himself. Not only that, but he has said some very harsh things about the Chinese government. My husband and I have done business with the Chinese and we've found that

Chapter 3

they have been very generous to us. I don't know why Trumpet has to be so mean to them. They're just trying to live the American dream like everyone else."

Bash: "What about you, Congressman Shifty?"

Shifty: "Well, Vaina, I have to agree with Diane, your hair *is* magnificent and I also love your lip gloss. Is that Laura Mercer Dessert Lip Glaze by any chance?"

Bash: "Why, yes, it is. How did you know?"

Shifty: "I use it to accentuate my lips just before I go on the air for an interview."

Bash: "I also use a serum plumper on my lips to give them a more fuller appearance."

Shifty: "I'll have to try that."

Bash: "So what's your take on the election results Congressman?"

Shifty: "Oh, there's no doubt Trumpet cheated. He called his friends in the Kremlin and had them hack into our system and change all the votes in his favor. I have definite proof."

Bash: "Really? What proof do you have?"

Shifty: "I have a anonymous source that works in the Moscow Pizza Hut. He says he knows a guy, who knows a guy, who knows another guy who knows computers and hacks into stuff all the time. He's pretty sure he hacked into our voting machines and changed most of the votes so that Trumpet would win."

Bash: "If that's true, that could be a bombshell!"

Shifty: "Yes, and it could also be a clam shell since it happened overseas. Get it? Clam shell, overseas?"

Bash: "Yes, I get it, Congressman. Why would the Russians want Trumpet to win? I thought they had a good relationship with Hillery."

Shifty: "Trumpet paid them off. I have proof."

Bash: "You have copies of money transfers?"

Shifty: "No, I have another anonymous source that says he knows a guy, who knows a guy, who knows a banker who said he saw the money transfers. I asked him for copies but he said that unfortunately his pet Siberian tiger ate them."

Bash: "Oh, that's too bad."

Shifty: "Yes, it is, but I have other proof."

Bash: "What is that?"

Shifty: "My mother happens to be psychic and she said he cheated."

Bash: "Wow! I'd like to interview your mother."

Shifty: "Uh, unfortunately, she died. But she told me Trumpet cheated before she passed away."

Bash: "Oh, I'm very sorry for your loss."

Shifty: "Don't be. She was a pain in the (bleep) while she was living but she had good psychic ability."

Bash: "Well, thank you Senator Finestine and Congressman Shifty for your informative remarks."

Bash shuffled a few papers and said, "There you have it, folks. Indisputable proof that Donald Trumpet cheated to win the election."

****

A few days later, Chris Steel took his dossier to his long time handling agent in the FBI. A man by the name of Mike Gata, who also used the alias of Al E. Gata.

"Steel! Long time no see," Gata greeted him, as Steel entered his office and took off the two pairs of sunglasses he had on, a long blonde wig, and fake beard.

"Nice disguise," Gata commented.

"Yeah, I got them at Wallmart," Steel replied.

"What can I do for you, Chris?"

Steel opened up the briefcase with him causing a

Chapter 3

canister of tear gas to go off, sending a small cloud rising up into the air.

"Cough! Cough!" Steel hacked, hurrying and putting on a gas mask he had in his pocket. "Damn! I forgot to put in the secret combination," he mumbled, waving away the gas cloud.

By then, Gata had also donned a gas mask and turned on a ventilation fan. "There won't be any more gas problems, will there, Steel?"

"Well, I did have Mexican for lunch... oh, you mean tear gas problems."

"Yes, Steel," Gata replied brusquely, turning off the fan and taking off his mask since the gas had dissipated. "Now what are you here for?"

"I've got some information that shows Trumpet in bed with the Russians to affect the election."

Gata's attention was riveted on Steel like a teenage boy looking at pornography. "How many Russians was the pervert in bed with?"

Steel shook his head. "I didn't mean literally, I meant he had a deal with the Russians to help him win the election and a campaign adviser named Carder Page met with Russian officials in Moscow."

"Oh, perfect! The FBI Director has been looking for something to charge Trumpet with."

"There's also a report in the dossier that Trumpet's foreign policy advisor during his campaign had information about the Russians acquiring Clinkton's emails he didn't divulge."

"Old news, Steel. Comby's already looked into it and started an investigation called *Crossfire Tornado*."

"Well, look through the dossier and see if there's anything else that might incriminate Trumpet. I'll take a copy to Bruce Odohr, the deputy AG since his wife is helping me," Steel stated as he stood up to leave, accidentally breaking wind.

Gata waved him away and put his gas mask back on.

After Steel's meeting with Bruce Odohr, it wasn't long before the information made it to Obahma's desk and was leaked to the Washington Compost, New York Grimes, and Ma Jones magazine.

Headlines read:

"Trumpet Has Affair With Star of The Thirty Year Old Virgin!" "Why, he should be excommunicated! That wasn't even a good movie, I mean, I heard it wasn't a good movie." Senator Mitt Rotney commented.

"Trumpet's Son-in-law Buys Russian Cossack Hats!" "Why doesn't he buy Chinese? They'll keep you a lot warmer on a cold night," Representative Eric Swallowell commented.

"Melonia Trumpet Speaks Italian, A Close Neighbor of Russia!" "Wah wah wah, wah wah wah wah wah," Representative Maxcine Wahwahs commented.

Shortly after that, Obahma met with the German Chancellor and poured gasoline onto the fire.

"Do you really need the flames that high to cook bratwurst?" the Chancellor's interpreter asked Obahma, as he stood in front of the firepit with singed eyebrows.

"Yes," (cough) I do," Obahma replied. "They need to be good and black. And while we're here, tell the Chancellor I just wanted her to know that Mr. Trumpet knew that the Russians were engaged in malicious cyber attacks that helped him win the election and made Hillery look like a vindictive wife bent on destroying all the women her husband had an affair with."

Her interpreter interpreted.

Chapter 3

The German Chancellor "Ached" and "Ya'd" a few words which her interpreter translated.

"Ze Chancellor said, 'If the Russians vanted someone to vin, it vould have been Clinkton and not Trumpet. They treasure the Re-set button she gave them.'"

Obahma laughed. "Ha! The joke's on them. It doesn't work and they must have found that out. 'Hell hath no fury like a Russki scorned.'"

"Don't you mean, 'Hell hath no fury like a voman scorned?'" Marbel's interpreter asked.

"Po-tay-toes, po-tah-toes," Obahma remarked.

But Obahma wasn't finished stoking the flames, metaphorically speaking this time. He expelled thirty-five Russian laundromats from the U.S. as retaliation for the alleged cyberattacks carried out by Russia. He then called in the Director of the Central Interrogation Agency, John Brinen, a short man with closely-cropped gray hair that had a permanent scowl even when he was smiling.

"You wanted to see me, Sir?" Brinen said, wearing a large "I Voted For Obahma" button on his lapel.

"Yes, Brinen. Take a chair."

"Where do you want it, Sir?" Brinen asked.

"Sit down, Director," Obahma growled impatiently.

"Will do, Mr. President. Is there a reason you wanted to see me?"

"Yes, Brinen, I always have a reason for seeing people. I'm tasking everyone in the intelligence services to come to the same conclusion that Pootin interfered with the election to help Trumpet win. You'll be coordinating with the VP, Comby, McCave, and Pzok to support this position. Am I clear?"

"Clear as a psycho killer's conscience," Brinen replied. "But does the VP have to be involved too? You know he gets easily confused."

"You're right. Scratch him off the list and just work with the others."

Brinen thumped his chest with his fist and said, "Your wish is my command, Mr. President."

"Good. Now scram."

Brinen bowed down then left, mumbling something about needing to change his adult diaper.

****

Days before Trumpet's inauguration, the outgoing administration was supposed to share their daily briefs with the incoming administration but they didn't. Obahma's excuse was that they were still in the wash machine. At least that was what Dennis McDonut, Obahma's Chief of Staff, told Trumpet's aides.

Steve Cannon, Trumpet's Chief Strategist, was extremely irate and called Obahma's Chief of Staff. McDonut answered, chewing on a maple bar.

"McDonut!" Cannon thundered, causing McDonut to look out the window to see if it was raining.

"This is Steve Cannon. I just found out about a report you guys have that implicates Trumpet with some Russian collusion bullsh#%. I want to see it."

There was a brief pause on the line as McDonut stuffed the other half of the maple bar in his mouth, then he said, "I'mph afraid that won't... 'Smack, smack,' be possible, Steve. "Gulp!" "Obahma's dog ate it and it's irretrievable. That is, of course, you want to dig through a pile of dog crap."

"Don't give me that crap," Cannon roared. "Wait! Maybe I do want the crap."

"I'm sorry," McDonut replied, "but we already sent it to the dump." He then heard what sounded like a dying

―――――――――――― Chapter 3 ――――――――――――

water buffalo on the other end of the line.

"Uh, Steve... tell you what. Why don't I have the directors of the unintelligence and federal law enforcement agencies meet with Trumpet and brief him on their, uh, findings. I'm afraid that's the best I can offer."

Cannon rattled off a string of expletives that would have made Hugh Heftner blush, then finally said, "All right, I guess that will have to do, but I'm not happy about it."

"I'll let the directors know," McDonut promised. Hanging up, he put his thumbs in his ears and fluttered his fingers, saying, "Na, na, na, na, na, na," to the phone as if it were Cannon.

****

John Brinen, Director of the **Central Interrogation Agency**, James Claptrapper, Director of the **National Unintelligence Agency**, Mickey (The Mouse) Rogers, Director of the **National Insecurity Agency**, and Jim Comby, very tall Director of the **Federal Bureau of Intimidation** entered the back door of Trumpet Tower and started up the stairs to the conference room on the eighty-fifth floor. Three were disguised as elderly grandmas and one was dressed like a boy scout to avoid recognition. Comby looked like the Jolly Green Giant with three Munchkins.

"How many more of these *&%#^! stairs are there? These heels are killing me and my wig keeps falling off!" Claptrapper growled as they arrived at the third floor.

"If you weren't such an old fart and went to the gym once in awhile, these stairs wouldn't be so bad," Brinen commented, breathing just as hard.

Claptrapper, with his chunky face and medium build, gave him an incredulous look. "*You* go to the gym?"

"No, but I do ten squat thrusts every day," Brinen replied.

Comby chuckled as he combed his hair. "I use the StairMaster. Ever heard of it?"

Between huffing and puffing, Rogers declared, "I've heard of the Stair Master. It's Richard Simmuns... isn't it?"

"No," Brinen interjected, "I think it's Jane Fondue. I'd exercise with her any day."

"The StairMaster is an exercise machine," Comby stated with a deadpan look.

"I'd say Fondue is an exercise machine," Brinen stated with a twinkle in his eye. "Ever see her do squat thrusts?"

Rogers gave a lecherous chuckle and Claptrapper wiped the drool from his mouth.

Twenty-five floors later, the four men reached their destination. Claptrapper wheezed like a pneumonia patient on a ventilator, Brinen's face was the color of a red globe on a stoplight, Rogers snorted in rapid succession like a bull about to charge, and Comby, being the youngest of all four, bounced up and down with his arms in the air.

Claptrapper threw one of his heels at him for showing off.

Comby put it in his backpack and said, "Now I'm going to keep it."

The four men walked up to the entrance of the conference room, guarded by two large shirtless secret service agents in tight shorts who could have been mistaken for professional wrestlers with machine guns, and showed their credentials. After the guards frisked them, they entered the well-fortified room through a thick steel door and noticed a shallow, flat-bottomed open boat with *Donald's Skiff* written on the side, taking up most of the room. Trumpet sat behind a desk on the bow wearing a captain's hat and faced the door they came in. He looked at the three elderly unintelligence chiefs, who were gasping for

Chapter 3

air, and said, "We have oxygen if you need it, ladies."

Claptrapper took the wig off his dome-shaped bald head and wheezed, "No, but I'll take a shot of bourbon if ya got it."

"Sorry, I don't drink," Trumpet declared.

Rogers mumbled, "You will after dealing with these knuckleheads a few months."

"Permission to come aboard?" Comby asked.

"Permission granted," Trumpet replied.

The four men walked up the gangplank and stood before Trumpet, who motioned to a bench in front of his desk and said, "Have a seat, and don't mind the fish smell. I just had some sardine hors d'oeuvres and the odor kind of lingers."

Brinen, Rogers, and Claptrapper sat down, but Comby strode over and stood next to Trumpet.

"Don't you want to sit with your comrades?" Trumpet asked him.

"That's a term the Russians use for friend, isn't it?" Comby asked.

"I don't know, I don't have any Russian friends just business associates," Trumpet replied.

Comby turned away and put his Buzz Lightgear transmitter watch to his mouth. "Trumpet said he had Russian associates," he whispered, then turned back to Trumpet and said, "I think I'm good right here."

Claptrapper then wrinkled his nose to match the rest of his face, and said, "I suppose introductions are in order. I am James Claptrapper, Director of National Unintelligence, the man next to me is John Brinen, Director of the Central Interrogation Agency, the man next to him is Mickey Rogers, Director of the National Insecurity Agency, and the boy scout next to you is Jim Comby,

Federal Bureau of Intimidation Director."

Suddenly, an alarming growl pierced the air.

"And that would be my stomach growling," Claptrapper added.

Trumpet turned to his wife, standing on the other side of him, and said, "Melonia, why don't you bring in some refreshments." She frowned at the inference of being referred to as a servant and started to leave.

Brinen, Rogers, and Claptrapper all held up their hands and said, "No sardine hors d'oeuvres, please."

"Bring something else," Trumpet informed his wife.

A moment later, she returned with a bowl of pretzels and small plastic cups of ginger ale.

Rogers snidely commented, "Wow! This is just like flying on Northwest Airlines... not that I would *fly* commercial."

Trumpet chuckled and said, "Those are quite the disguises. I would never have guessed you were men. Are those outfits comfortable?"

Brinen replied, "I could get used to it."

Claptrapper leaned over to him and whispered, "These ladies panties are riding up in my crotch."

Brinen smiled and said, "I'm not wearing any."

Melonia suddenly noticed that Claptrapper had only one high heel on. In her thick European accent, she asked, "Vould you like me to bring you a new pair of shoos? I have three hoondred pairs."

"No, Dear," Claptrapper replied in his best grandma voice, "I find that just wearing one heel at a time gives my other foot a welcomed rest. In fact, it's time to switch to the other now."

He took off the heel and began screwing it onto his other foot. After struggling with it for a moment, he fi-

Chapter 3

nally forced it on as best he could. Smiling painfully, he said, "There. Now my other little piggies can get a rest."

Melonia put her finger to her chin and said, "I must try that."

"Thanks, honey, you can go now," Trumpet instructed her. He then turned to Comby and said, "Were you really a boy scout?"

"I was an eagle scout," Comby corrected him sarcastically, looking down his nose at Trumpet as if he had been called a girl scout.

Turning to the other three directors, Trumpet clasped his hands together and sat back in his captain's chair. "So, what kind of information do you have for me?" he asked.

Comby whipped out a thick folder from his backpack that had "*Extremely Confidential Material for the President Elect's Eyes Only, Unauthorized Use is Strictly Prohibited and Violators Will Be Shot,*" stamped in bold letters and handed it to Trumpet.

Slowly opening the official-looking folder, Trumpet started to read the material when Comby quickly turned the pages of Steel's dossier and said, "You can skip over that part, the more interesting information is what you'll really want to read."

"Oh," Trumpet remarked and thumbed through pages until Comby nodded. He then began to read about a meeting that was recorded as part of an investigation into a possible spy ring in the NBA.

"*Saturday, January 17, 2015 at 9:22 p.m.*

Meeting between Coach Lionel Hollings and Brooklyn Nets owner, Joe Tsigh. Location: a Manhattan condo tower penthouse.

The conversation went as follows:

Tsigh to Hollings: "How is the team doing?" (*possible*

meaning: "Have our Russian special forces made any headway in eliminating top U.S. government officials?")

Hollings to Tsigh: "They're doing about as well as can be expected with the injuries to key players we've had. (possible meaning: "A few have been wounded as a result of firefights they were involved in. It will take awhile for them to recover, unfortunately.")

Tsigh to Hollings: "Well, other players will have to step up. See that they do or our investors will be very unhappy." (possible meaning: "The remaining squad will have to fill in. Take care of it or Moscow will have both our heads.")

Hollings to Tsigh: "Don't worry, I'll have three a day practices if needed in order to get the backups playing at a higher caliber." (possible meaning: "I'll make sure they have extra target practice and use higher caliber weapons.")

After Trumpet read the dossier, a grim look crawled across his face. "Russian spies are a serious matter, especially if they've infiltrated the NBA," he commented.

Comby pointed to the dossier and said, "Make sure you read the account of the prostitutes in the hotel where Obahma once slept."

Trumpet looked it over and said, "Hey, I've stayed at that hotel and no one ever told me they had prostitutes or I would have gone back." He then nervously looked around and said, "Whew! It's a good thing I sent Melonia out or I'd be sleeping in the guest room, which really isn't that bad come to think of it."

All four unintelligence directors made a note of it.

****

Nancy Lugosi opened the lid from the inside and rose up from the coffin-like bed, her rigid body resembling a slow catapult. Making sure the shades were closed, she stepped out then slowly trudged toward the

Chapter 3

bathroom and clapped her hands for the red-bulbed light to come on.

Approaching the sink, she looked in the mirror but could see no reflection. It cracked anyway.

"Damn!" she cursed. "I'll have to replace another mirror. Oh well, I've got enough money to buy a million mirrors from my insider stock trading, what am I worried about?"

Smacking her lips, she could still taste the Bin and Jarry's marrow-flavored ice cream she had for a midnight snack. She preferred the hemoglobin-flavored ice cream but her absent-minded slave, er, husband had forgotten to pick some up at the store. After sharpening her canine teeth and spraying on way too much perfume called "Born to kill," she went to her dresser, ran her skeletal fingers through her hair and slipped on a black dress that had a plunging neckline down to her belly button. "When you got 'em, flaunt 'em," she hummed. She was the House Majority Leader and had a busy day ahead of her. After painting her dagger-like nails a color called *Black Death* and putting on a crimson-colored lipstick, she went into the kitchen and opened the monstrous refrigerator. Pouring a few ounces of what appeared to be tomato juice in a glass, she added some Worcestershire sauce, celery salt, horseradish, and filled the rest of the glass with vodka. Taking a big sip, she said, "There's nothing like a real Bloody Mary to start your day." She then melted into the finely upholstered kitchen chair and smiled wickedly. "Who shall I put the bite on today?" she quietly said as an emaciated-looking cat sauntered in and jumped up on her lap.

"And how are we today, My Little Precious," she cooed, petting the hairless feline as it dug its claws into her leg, drawing formaldehyde.

Picking up her mobile phone, she went to her email and looked at the various messages. "Hmmm," she mused, "here's one from Hillery Clinkton marked 'Urgent.' She probably wants a job now that she's out on her tookus."

The email read:

"Nancy,

I've begun a campaign to get Trumpet out of the White House and I need your help. Would you be willing to initiate a special counsel investigation into the Russian interference in our election and Trumpet's participation in colluding with them? I know you hate the man as much as I do and would love to see the misogynist bas#@rd hung by his oversized tie from the White House flagpole. I have a dossier that would all but guarantee his impeachment you can use. Just appoint an Autocratic staff so the results are in our favor. I'll send you the dossier I have by FedX so be watching for it. Hogs and quiches...Hillery"

Nancy took another sip of her drink and cackled like a witch in a cauldron factory. Impeaching Trumpet wouldn't be a problem once the Autocrats had a majority in the House, but the Rebubbacans had a majority in the Senate. More than likely they would acquit, but she still might convince enough RHINOs (Rebubbacan Hacks In Name Only) to vote her way when the time came. She would just have to see, but the dossier wouldn't be enough. She needed some incident to provide an excuse for the special counsel to be initiated, whether it was valid or not. She would have to let her minions close to Trumpet know to be on the lookout for the right ingredients that would make a good impeachment cobbler.

"Dum de dum de dumpet. We're going to impeach Trumpet," she trilled as she stroked her hairless cat.

Chapter 3

Trumpet Toot: With the Mexican cartels sneaking across our open southern border, we must build a wall. Mexico is going to either reimburse us or pay for it some other way.

Headline in the Washington Grimes: *Trumpet says Mexico will pay for a wall on the southern border. Mexican President agrees as long as it's built with Legos.*

Chapter Four
"Hell to the Thief"

Streter Pzok entered Jim Comby's office, making sure his fly was zipped up this time, and asked, "You wanted to see me, J. Edgar?"

"What? Oh, yes, Agent Rising Star. I need to leak something to the press," Comby replied.

"Should I get a container, Sir?"

Comby looked at him with listless eyes. "No, Pzok. Fax this report to Buzzard Feed and put 'Attention: Noel Scrupels.' Then make a copy and give it to Obahma. Any questions?"

"No, Sir, I'll get right on it." Pzok took the report, bowed and left.

As he walked down the hall, he thought, "If only Clinkton had won the election, I would have received a raise and could have bought the yacht I put a down payment on. Oh well, '*The Resistance*' can still destroy the orange ogre."

Returning to his office, he faxed the report as ordered and was about to take the copy to Obahma when Leesa Page stormed into his office.

"Leesa! What's the matter?" he asked, as his paramour with her long face and short forehead entered.

"Oooo, oooo, that imbecilic misogynistic megalomaniac has gone too far," she ranted, as her dark eyes flashed. She tossed her long, straight brown hair back, pushed him in his chair, and plopped down on his lap.

"Are you referring to Trumpet?"

"No, I'm referring to Bozo the Clown, and please use another pronoun."

"Oh, sorry, but Trumpet and Bozo the Clown are

Chapter 4

one of the same."

"Whatever," she replied with a snarl.

"What's got you so upset?" Pzok asked.

"What's got me so UPSET?" she shrieked, accentuating the last word. "The new Demander-in-Chief just announced the first thing he's going to do when he gets into the oval office is freeze all bureaucrat salaries!"

Pzok made a face and said, "That idiot. Celery tastes awful when it's frozen."

"NOT CELERY, SALARIES! ARE YOU @%$#&* DEAF?"

"No need to be vulgar unless we're... you know," Pzok remarked, attempting to placate her. "But not to worry. We'll have Bozo out of Office before you can say "Jack Sprat could eat no fat, his wife could eat no lean, and so betwixt them both you see..."

Page rolled her eyes. "I get it, I get it. Why do you always have to belabor the point."

"You said 'you.'"

"So did...never mind. We need to come up with a plan to get rid of that hamburger-eating twit before he gets rid of every progressive thing we've been able to accomplish."

Pzok furrowed his brow and said, "Aren't you taking this a bit too seriously?"

"No, I'm not, and stop saying 'you!'" she growled.

"Sorry, this new pronoun thing is confusing," he replied, scrunching his face until he looked like a squashed marshmallow.

"Well, we better do something soon before he has us all driving gas-powered SUV's. Are you coming by our secret apartment this evening? I told my husband I'm working late again."

"I can't make it tonight, my ten-year-old daughter has a school dance recital. They're doing Swan Lake in the nude."

"Well, it's nice to see our schools' curriculum is still progressive." She then went into "lovey-dovey" mode and asked, "So, what did the Director have to say to my handsome Chief of Counterespionage?"

"Oh, he just wanted me to run an errand. He's even calling me Agent Rising Star now."

She raised her eyebrows. "Rising Star? Sounds like a Native American name. Elizabeth Warner is part Cherakee she claims."

"I didn't know that. But she certainly has the features-blonde hair, pure white skin, ha, ha."

"She even drives a Cherakee, which personally I think is politically incorrect and a misappropriation of the tribal name, but she's an Autocrat, so it's okay."

Leesa rubbed the bald spot on the back of Pzok's head and said, "Well, I had better go back to my office before people start to talk about us."

"I think it's too late for that," he retorted. "You left my door open."

"Oops!" she exclaimed and hurried out with a girlish grin.

Streter Pzok just shook his head and mumbled, "I'm glad she didn't stick her tongue in my ear. Now what was I going to do before she came in? Oh, yeah. Take a copy to Obahma."

Shortly after he dropped off the report as ordered, Obahma called four people into his office for a last minute diabolical plan. The first person he summoned was Joe Hiden, his VP.

"B-Buh...B-Buh.." Joe stammered, then finally said,

Chapter 4

"Mr. President. You wanted to, uh... what did you want?"

"To see you, Joe," Obahma replied.

"Oh, yes, that's why I came," Hiden chuckled.

"I've got a few others coming so have a seat," Obahma said, pointing to a wheelchair.

Comby walked in just then and gave a scout salute.

"Who else is coming," Joe asked, popping a wheely in his chair and breaking wind at the same time. "Squeaky seat," he remarked with a guilty look.

Comby leered at him like Joe had just eaten a mouthful of cat litter.

"Susan and Sally," Obahma replied.

"Ah, the SS," Joe commented, holding one arm out straight and putting his index finger under his nose with the other.

When Susan Ryce and Sally Yaytz finally arrived, Obahma began the meeting by saying, "What I'm about to tell you doesn't leave this room."

"You mean we have to stay here forever?" Hiden asked.

"No, Joe, just what I tell you," Obahma replied, slowly and succinctly, like he was talking to a child.

Hiden smiled and said, "Oh, yeah, I thought that's what you meant." He then looked around the room and tried to remember why he was there.

Obahma continued. "Look, a lot of information is going to come to me about Donald Trumpet. Information that we hope will get him impeached. I'll pass it on to you and I want you to make sure you look at everything and put the right people on it."

Hiden raised his hand.

"Yes, Joe?"

"Excuse me, but wouldn't you rather have us put

people on the left on it rather than the right?"

Obahma put his hand on his forehead, mumbling "I should have picked Tim Cane for Vice President." Using his patronizingly persuasive voice, he said, "Tell you what, Joe. Why don't you sit this one out."

"Is this chair okay?" Hiden asked.

Obahma sighed. "Okay, everybody out! You too, Joe!" he commanded, shooing them away like flies.

After they left, Obahma walked out of the office and turned to his personal assistant and trainer, Reggie Luv. "Hey Reggie! Call Mike Flinn in will you and put me down for some one on one with you this evening."

"You got it, Boss Man."

A few minutes later, Flinn walked in. He had that look of a wimpy kid that bullies like to beat up and make fun of. "Michael T. Flinn reporting as ordered, Sir!" Flinn announced, in his shrill voice.

"Have a seat, Mike." Obahma snarled, with a tone as cold as a mole rat in the Arctic.

"Anything wrong, Mr. President?" Flinn asked, watching his breath come out in the suddenly cold room.

"Yes, something *is*, Mike," Obahma replied, raising his big eyebrows. "I understand you called Sergey Kissayak the Russian ambassador. Can you tell me why you called him?"

"Actually, Sir, he called me. He wanted to see if I knew the reason why you expelled thirty-five of his country's laundromats. I told him it was probably because the whites weren't white enough."

"We shouldn't be talking to the Russians right now since they interfered with our election. Are you sure that's all you talked about?"

"Well, he did ask what you wanted for your birthday

and I told him you mentioned that you'd like a twelve million dollar mansion in Martha's Vineyard."

"That was confidential just between us, Mike. I'm sorry, but you're fired for leaking classified information."

"But..."

"No excuses, clean out your desk and leave the White House. I have a transition to prepare for."

Flinn stood up and gave a one fingered salute, wheeled about and marched out mumbling, "I hope your mansion has termites."

Obahma took a quick glance at the upcoming commitments on his Saul Alinski's favorite propaganda sayings desk calendar and said, "Oh @#%&! Trumpet's inauguration is tomorrow and it's customary for the incumbent President to attend. I'll have to cancel my speech to the *Girls Needing Radical Change* group."

****

The next day, people started filing into the western front of the U.S. Capitol facing the National Mall with files handed out by the Aces Hardware Lobbyists. There was quite a police presence including bum-sniffing dogs and national guardspersons with salt and pepper spray since Black Lives Madder threatened to riot. Once all the invitees had seated themselves and Trumpet took his place on the podium, the inaugural ceremony began. After opening remarks by Senator Ray Blunt, Ted Newgent played a hard rock version of "America the Beautiful." Unfortunately, he was the only performer Trumpet could book who was conservative and available. Mike Pensive was then sworn in as V.P. and afterwards, Trumpet took the oath as the President of the United States. The band made up of hip-hop musicians chosen specifically by Obahma then played a rap version of *Hail to the Chief* called *Hell to the Thief.*

> *Hell to the Thief some have chosen for the nation,*
> *Hell to the Thief! We despise him, one and all*
> *Hell to the Thief, we don't pledge cooperation*
> *In the fulfillment of a sad, lousy call*
> *Yours is the aim to make this grand country much worse,*
> *This you will do, That's our strong, firm belief*
> *Hell to the one some selected as commander,*
> *Hell to the racist dude! Hell to the Thief!*

After they had finished, Trumpet went up to the lectern and gave the band a dirty look. He then gave his inaugural speech.

After thanking a few dignitaries, he promised to give the power back to the people the administration had taken from them, which caused Obahma to give *him* a dirty look, but received a few cheers from the Rebubbacans. He then went on to say how all the politicians in D.C. had prospered while the people hadn't. Even the Rebubbacans gave him a dirty look. He continued.

"All that changes once I take office because the United States of America is your country." He then went into a rousing and slightly off key rendition of "*This is My Country*" changing the words to "*This is Your Country*" which caused a few dogs to howl in the distance.

He then continued his speech by promising to make changes in several fields, baseball, football, and soccer (to name a few) and said from now on he would put America first when it came to choosing the type of cuisine he would eat, and he would close the borders to illegal aliens and the skies to extraterrestrial aliens. He ended by saying, "Together, we will *Make America Terrific Again!*" then he asked for God to bless America and Tiny Tim. A

Chapter 4

priest, a rabbi, and a cardinal then gave the benedictions. Well, the rabbi and priest did, the cardinal just chirped. Then came the post inaugural ceremony events-a luncheon with food provided by Burger Emperor to be held at Stationary Hall; a parade of old military veterans with walkers (it lasted a long time); and a few Inaugural balls autographed by professional jugglers. It was slightly different from the usual post ceremony events.

****

When Donald Trumpet entered the oval office the next day to officially take over, Obahma stood up and said, "Here he comes, Mr. America! Come in Donny boy and I'll give you some last minute briefs."

"I prefer boxers, and that's Donald," Trumpet said.

Obahma smiled patronizingly with his chiseled features and said, "Well, when you sit in the President's chair you can wear whatever you want."

"Actually, I brought my own chair," Trumpet remarked.

Opening his briefcase, he pulled out what looked like an inflatable mattress and turned on the valve. When it had fully inflated, it resembled an ornate high-backed chair studded with fake jewels. He sat down on it and said, "What do you think? I got this at Thrones-R-Us for fifty bucks."

Obahma looked up at his eyebrows then said, "It might be just a tad bit too ostentatious for the Oval Office, but you're the king, er, President now."

"Any last minute advice?" Trumpet asked, sitting down on his newly inflated chair which immediately began to sound like a hummingbird breaking wind.

"Yes," Obahma replied. "I heard you're considering Mike Flinn as your National Insecurity Advisor."

"I am," Trumpet replied, studying Obahma as if he were a snake oil salesman.

"Bad idea," Obahma said, shaking his head slowly as if he was vacuuming with his nose.

"Why do you say that?" Trumpet asked, sinking deeper in his inflatable throne.

"Mike's a leaker," Obahma replied.

Trumpet looked at his chair and said, "Apparently this chair is too. What do you mean Mike is a leaker? Does he have to go to the bathroom alot?"

Obahma rolled his eyes up like a newspaper and said, "Sometimes he says things to other people that shouldn't leave this room. Classified things."

Trumpet lifted his head slightly. "That's not good."

"But, not to worry. I'm sure everything will run smoothly for you just like in all your lawsuits. I don't have anything else. Any questions?"

"None that I can think of at the moment," Trumpet replied. "I'll have a talk with Mike. I'm sure he'll come to

Chapter 4

see things my way. You know, the old Sinatra song, '*I Did It My Way*.'"

"Yes," Obahma smiled, thinking "Of course you'd pick a honky song." He turned serious and said, "Oh, there is one last thing before I leave."

"What's that?" Trumpet asked, as he sunk further down in the slowly deflating chair.

"I have an appointment with some *Black Lives Madder* people who want to meet with me now. It would probably be better if you weren't here when they come, since they seem to compare you to the Grand Lizard of the Ku Kluck Klan."

"I agree, that could be bad," Trumpet stated.

"Agreeing with the boss is a good habit to get into," Obahma remarked. He then pointed at Trumpet and said, "You might want to pass that along to your cabinet."

"Oh, I don't talk to furniture," Trumpet stated, sinking further into the seat. Now just his head and shoulders were looking out over his knees.

Obahma gave him a blank stare. "I was referring to the people you choose for your administrative cabinet."

"Why didn't you *say that*? A good leader should be clear in what he says," Trumpet remarked, as the chair continued to sink further.

Obahma gave Trumpet a zombie look and started toward him with his hands out in a choking position. Before he could reach him, Trumpet's head disappeared into the chair and only his two feet were sticking up.

"Uh, I think I'll need to return this chair. Could you help me out?" Trumpet uttered, holding up one hand.

Obahma hesitated for a moment to see if his replacement would hopefully suffocate.

"A little help, please!" Trumpet shouted louder.

Obahma smirked, then grudgingly grabbed Trumpet's arm and pulled him out.

"Thanks, Buhrock. I thought I was going to be eaten by the vinyl monster." Trumpet chuckled.

With a straight face, Obahma said, "It's too bad that you didn't get... a better chair. Here, I'll show you out."

After Trumpet left, Obahma pushed a button on his intercom/telephone system for his secretary.

"Yes, sir?"

"Get me Comby on the line."

"Right away, sir."

A second later, the FBI director came on the line. "Comby here."

"This is the President. Have you set up the wiretap on the oval office phone yet, Jim?"

"Yes, Mr. President. It's all ready to go."

"Good. Record everything... of course after I leave."

"Will do, Mr. President."

Obahma hung up and muttered, "Destroying this buffoon is going to be easier than negotiating with Iran to release American hostages, and it won't cost the taxpayers 400 million dollars."

****

The next day, Trumpet began picking his cabinet. He got a great deal at Ickea, then he started choosing the people for his administration. He needed a Chief of Staff immediately, so he picked Prince Riebus, who gleefully accepted. After Trumpet appointed him, Riebus left the Oval Office and danced down the hall, singing, "The Chief of Staff, the Chief of Staff, yes I am, the Chief of Staff."

After a few more appointments, Donald Trumpet sat down at the absolute desk in the Oval Office and ran both hands across the top like it was a new car. His eyes

Chapter 4

went misty for a moment then his stomach growled which brought him back to reality. He hadn't had breakfast yet and he could eat an Autocrat. Turning his attention to the telephone/intercom system, he pushed a button to contact his secretary. Immediately, lights in the room began to flash and a voice came on the speaker announcing, "Going to DefCon 5!"

"#@%&," Trumpet cursed. He pushed the button again and the voice said, "Terminating DefCon 5."

"These buttons all look the same," Trumpet muttered. Pushing another one, he held his breath until his secretary came on.

"Yes, Mr. President?"

"Oh, good. Maddy, find Riebus and tell him to pick up my breakfast at Burger Emperor. I want two triple sausage and egg sourdough breakfast sandwiches, a giant order of fries, and a Diet Koke. Also have him get a copy of the Compost."

"Yes, Mr. President."

A short while later, Riebus strode down the hall with a Burger Emperor sack in one hand and a Washington Compost newspaper in the other.

Sean Spicey, who Trumpet chose as his White House Press Secretary, chuckled as he passed.

Riebus whirled around and snapped, "What are you laughing at?"

Spicey turned, wiping the grin off his face along with some leftover jam from a peanut butter and jelly sandwich he just had in the White House commissary to celebrate his appointment as Press Secretary. "Looks like you went to Burger Emperor," he stated, stifling a snicker.

"How did you know?" Riebus asked, looking at Spicey with one eye cocked.

Spicey pointed and said, "You're wearing a Burger Emperor crown."

Riebus looked down his nose at Spicey and said, "It was free and besides, I do have royal blood."

"Really? And what royal blood flows through your veins, Prince?"

With a haughty expression, Riebus turned up his chin and replied, "I have been drinking Royal Coronet Cola every day since I was a child. I'm sure much of it is flowing through my veins as we speak."

"All right, Your Majesty," Spicey remarked, continuing on his way.

Straightening his cardboard crown with a lopsided smirk, Riebus carried on to deliver Trumpet's breakfast and his newspaper. Glancing at the front page headline on the Compost, he said, "NO!" out loud.

Marching up to the oval office with a scowl, he waited at the open doorway for Trumpet to beckon him in.

Trumpet noticed he was obviously distraught and waved him over to the desk.

"What's got your knickers in a twist?" Trumpet asked, as Riebus approached.

Riebus plunked the front page down on the desk and exclaimed, "Look at the headline in today's Compost, Chief!"

The headline read: ***"Trumpet has Alice Cooper Syndrome! Bites Heads off of Chickens According to Reliable Medical Sources in Haiti."***

Trumpet poked strongly at the headline with his index finger and exclaimed, "This is phony news! How can they print this! I've never bitten the head off a chicken. I bit the head off a gingerbread man when I was a kid, but never a chicken."

Chapter 4

"Do you want me to file a lawsuit against them?" Riebus asked.

"No, none of the major media outlets would carry it anyway and I want the people to know just how phony this is. I'll go on Tooter and send out a Toot denying the claim. I have a gazillion followers so the word will get out."

"That is an excellent idea, Chief. Here is your breakfast." Riebus handed him the bulging paper bag.

Opening the sack Trumpet asked, "Did you get two triple sausage and egg sourdough breakfast sandwiches?"

"Of course, and a giant order of fries."

"You know, when I starred on *The Adventist*, I could eat three of these and two giant orders of fries. But now that I'm President, I have to watch my salary intake."

"Don't you mean your calorie intake, Sir?"

"Never correct the boss," Trumpet said. Pushing a button on a large box on his desk, the front opened and a boxing glove shot out, hitting Riebus in the groin.

"You get one warning," Trumpet declared.

Doubling over, Riebus said in a high voice, "I think one warning is all I need, Chief."

"And stop calling me Chief. I'm not an Indian. The only person around here that claims to be, is Elizabeth "Pokeyhontas" Warner and she's about as Indian as the Queen of England," Trumpet growled. Where's my Diet Koke?"

Riebus scrunched his face and replied, "Uh, I'll get one out of the Presidential refrigerator."

"Hurry up, I don't want the newspapers to read, "President chokes on breakfast sandwich because the Chief of Staff forgot his Diet Koke. And take off that crown, it may give people the impression that you're in charge of the White House."

"But Sir, I just got this at Burger Emperor when I picked up your breakfast."

"Now, or you're fired," Trumpet warned.

Riebus rolled his eyes and reluctantly removed the cardboard crown with a pouty look.

As he hurried out the door, Trumpet shouted, "You never would have made it on *The Adventist*."

Once out of sight, Riebus stuck out his tongue and put the crown back on his head.

Trumpet chuckled to himself, "I knew my warning glove would come in handy." He looked at the paper again as he waited for his beverage and growled, "I'll just Toot a rebuttal to this garbage. I don't even know who Alice Cooper is!"

After he finished his lower calorie breakfast, he asked his secretary to call Comby and McCave and have them report to the Oval Office.

When the two agents arrived, Trumpet pointed to Comby from his patched inflated throne and said, "Hey, Jim. Sean Spicey told me you were investigating Mike Flinn. How come?"

"He's had secret conversations with Russian ambassador Sergey Kissayak," Comby promptly replied.

McCave nodded.

"What kind of secret conversations?" Trumpet asked, focusing a laser gaze at Comby, singeing his eyelids.

"That's uh, classified, Sir," Comby nervously replied.

"I'm the President now! You can tell me!" Trumpet bellowed, like a bull moose who accidentally walked into a convenience store.

McCave's eyebrows went up and he leaned toward Comby and whispered something.

Comby took an erect stance as if he was about to use

Chapter 4

the urinal. "If I told you, Sir, you wouldn't have plausible deniability. Besides, Flinn is too chummy with the Soviets so I had to launch an investigation. I call it *Crossfire Tornado*," Comby stated proudly.

"What do you mean he's too chummy with the Soviets?" Trumpet asked.

"Uh, he's talking to them?" Comby replied.

"So you're investigating him mainly because he talked to the Russians?"

"Well... yes."

"I think the FBI can spend their time better somewhere else than investigating people who talked to the Russians. Hell, even my son has talked to the Russians."

McCave whispered into his lapel pin, "Donald Trumpet Jr. also spoke with the Russians."

"If you want the investigation terminated on Flinn, Mr. President, then I'll be the terminator," Comby stated in his best Arnold Swartzenager voice.

"That's all I have, you're dismissed," Trumpet stated.

McCave and Comby turned to go in the same direction and bumped into each other. After righting themselves, they left.

"You're really not going to terminate the Flinn investigation, are you Director?" McCave asked.

"I am, but you're not," Comby replied.

****

Returning to his grotto, McCave called his secretary on the intercom. "Hey Mary."

"Yes, Mr. McCave?"

"That's Deputy Director McCave," he corrected her.

"Sorry, Deputy Director. What do you need, Sir?"

"Have Leesa Page report to me," he replied.

"Right away, Sir, uh, Deputy Director."

"That's better," McCave retorted, "I almost had to pistol whip you."

When Page learned McCave wanted to see her, she texted Pzok. "McCave wants to see me. What do you think he wants?" *Leesa*

"He probably just wants you to clean his Glock. It's your turn." *Streter*

"What if it's something else?" *Leesa*

"You worry too much. Wear a wire just in case. Come to my office and I'll attach it to your body." *Streter*

"Oooh, I can't wait." *Leesa*

After Pzok fastened the listening device and synched it to his mobile phone, Page left and entered McCave's grotto. "You wanted to see me, Sir?"

"That's Deputy Director," McCave snapped back. "Why doesn't anyone around here call me by my official title? Have a seat, Page. I have an errand I need you to run for me."

"What is it, Deputy Director, and could you please speak loudly into my necklace."

McCave gave her a wary eye and said, "I need you to leak some information to the Journal about the investigation I'm conducting on the Clinkton's Foundation."

Page appeared as surprised as a tree sloth that just laid an egg. "That's all?"

"Yes, just make sure you sign the tip 'Anonymous' when you fax it."

"You're really investigating the Clinkton Foundation, Sir, uh, Deputy Director?"

"Of course not, Betty Bimbo. It's just to make me look good."

"Oh, I see. I'll do it right away." She stood up to leave.

"Deputy Director," he reminded her.

Chapter 4

"Oh, yes, Deputy Director." She hurried out and once outside his office, she muttered, "Oh, yes, Deputy sh%*head."

"You're still being recorded," Pzok reminded in her ear piece. "Don't worry, I'll erase that last part."

****

The next day, Pzok's secretary came on his intercom and said, "Chief, the Deputy Director wants to see you in his office."

Pzok mumbled, "What does McCave want now? Okay, tell his secretary I'll be right there."

Just outside McCave's grotto, Pzok turned on his new and slightly modified Mission Improbable watch to 'record' and knocked on the door.

"Come in!" McCave called out.

Pzok entered and said, "You wanted to see me, Sir?"

"That's DEPUTY DIRECTOR! and no, your appearance repulses me. I just want you to take care of a little matter Obahma wanted handled."

"But he's not the President any more."

"I know that, you idiot. Obahma asked Comby to have Flinn destroyed, so I want you to interrogate Flinn and see if you can find something we can prosecute the #@%$&* on."

Pzok put on his best Norman Baits psycho smile and said, "Leave it to me, Sir, I'll have him confessing to the JFK assassination before I'm through."

McCave picked up a rifle leaning against his desk and said, "Speaking of the JFK assassination, have I showed you this baby?"

"Yes, you have," Pzok responded.

McCave ignored him and said, "It's the same rifle Ozwald used to shoot JFK. It's a 6.5×52mm Carcano

Model 38 infantry carbine with a telescopic sight. It's accurate at 200 yards." He pointed it at Pzok and dry-fired. "You'll have something back for me within the week, won't you, Pzok?"

Pzok swallowed hard and said, "Uh, will do, Deputy Director." He slowly backed up then left the office and turned off the recording on his watch. Returning to his own office, he took out his phone and texted Page.

"Hey Hot Stuff, you wanna help me interrogate Mike Flinn?" *Streter*

"Sure. Do we get to waterboard him?" *Leesa*

"No, that's CIA stuff. Maybe we can threaten his family and pets if he doesn't confess to something we can prosecute him for." *Streter*

"Sounds like a plan, Stan." *Leesa*

"Who's Stan? Are you seeing someone else?" *Streter*

"It's just a line from a song, you silly man." *Leesa*

"Oh. I'll text you when I call Flinn in. I'll just have to come up with something to get him here so he doesn't suspect what it's for." *Streter*

"I'm sure your brilliant mind will come up with something, Snuggy Wuggy. I'll be breathlessly awaiting your text." *Leesa*

The next day, FBI agents went to Flinn's house and told him the National Insecurity Department was going to throw him a surprise going away party and to accompany them to where the festivities were to take place.

Flinn was blindfolded and told to act surprised when they arrived. After taking him down a long hall, they removed the blindfold and opened a door.

Flinn looked around and said, "Isn't this kind of a small room for a surprise party and where's all the staff?"

One of the agents pushed him inside and said, "Sur-

Chapter 4

prise! Have a seat at the table."

Flinn sat down and looked around the 10' x 12' room. A large observation window on one wall had a sign above it saying, "THIS IS NOT AN OBSERVATION WINDOW." Another sign on the door read, *"Abandon all hope, ye who enter here."*

After an hour's wait, Pzok and Page entered the room and sat down across from him.

"I take it this isn't a surprise party for me," Flinn remarked.

Pzok turned on the recording unit and said, "Mister Flinn we have a few questions for you. Keep in mind you're under oath to tell the truth, cross your heart and hope to die."

"Yeah, and stick a needle in my eye. You learn that in FBI school?" Flinn asked.

Pzok smirked and said, "I'll ask the questions here. I have a recorded phone conversation between you and Russian ambassador Sergey Kissayak where you promised better relations between the U.S. and Russia if they interfered in our election. Do you deny it?" He then positioned a table lamp directly in Flinn's eyes.

Flinn squinted and replied, "I had a conversation with Kissayak about Trumpet having better relations with Russia than what Obahma had, but I never asked Kissayak to interfere in the election."

Pzok smiled and said, "Leesa, play the tape."

Page held up her mobile phone and pushed "Play." The following conversation was heard:

"Hello, Meester Mike Flinn, this is Sergey Kissayak. If Russia promises to rig the election for Donald Trumpet, how about relaxing some of the sanctions you have on us. Da?"

"Certainly, Mr. Kissayak. I'll tell the President-Elect and we'll take care of it."

Page turned off the recording and gave Flinn a smug smile, like she had just brought home a school paper with a gold star on it.

Flinn's face turned the color of undercooked brisket. "Kissayak never said that and I never promised that! That wasn't even my voice. It sounded more like her voice for mine and your voice for Kissayak's, if you ask me."

Page gave him a sneer and said, "Nobody's asking you."

Pzok turned the lamp's brightness up a notch. "So you deny talking with Kissayak."

"Yes, I mean we did have a conversation," Flinn responded, "but not that conversation."

Pzok smiled. "Your first response is that you denied talking with Ambassador Kissayak, so you lied. Admit you lied, Mr. Flinn, or I'll have agents arrest your wife, your kids, and your dog for being accessories to your crime."

Flinn realized he was trapped like a rat in a cat, up feces creek without a kayak, caught between a rock and a roll. He had no choice but to go along with whatever Pzok wanted him to admit to.

"All right, all right!" he cried. "I lied, so just leave my dog out of it."

Pzok turned off the recording, then he and Page stood up from the table.

Pzok pointed his finger at Flinn and said, "All right, Mr. Flinn, you can go but don't leave the country."

"Am I going to be charged with something?" Flinn asked.

Pzok smirked and said, "Probably lying to the FBI."

"And upsetting President Obahma," Page added,

Chapter 4

turning up her nose.

****

Later that evening, Trumpet opened his Presidential laptop with a campaign bumper sticker on the top that read, "Trumpet Gives a Toot About America."

"Let's see how the Compost likes these Toots," he muttered as he logged on and began typing.

"For the record, I do not bite the heads off chickens. I wouldn't mind biting the heads off a few reporters I know, however."

The next day, the Washington Compost and New York Grimes had headlines that respectively read: **"Trumpet Threatens to Kill Reporters!"** and **"Trumpet Calls Reporters Chickens and Threatens to Bite Their Heads off!"**

Chapter Five
Boss! Da Press! Da Press!

The Compost and Grimes were two of Trumpet's biggest print media critics, but other media publications and news outlets showed their bias toward him as well. A reporter for (*Once Upon A*) *Time Magazine* was allowed in the White House oval office and the first thing he noticed was that Trumpet had removed a bust of a famous civil rights leader. The next issue of the magazine had a tagline on the cover that said, "***Trumpet Removes Famous Civil Rights Leader's Bust From Oval Office.***"

The article went on to say the removal was due to Trumpet's racist attitudes toward people of color. What the reporter failed to notice was that the bust was sitting on a credenza behind him. Sherlock Homes would cer-

Chapter 5

tainly not have said, "Astute observation."

The next day, Trumpet held his first press conference to outline his plans for the nation and to answer a few questions from the press.

Taking the podium, he addressed the reporters. "Thanks for coming on such short notice, I wanted to let you all know what I'm planning for the country and what I've been able to accomplish since I've been in office. I'll answer any questions you might have afterwards. First, let me say I'm trying to get my administration chosen, which would be much easier if the Autocrats wouldn't keep stalling my nominations. I've managed to get rid of a few 'Never Trumpeters' and rather than rely on the press to report the facts, I'll be going on Tooter to let the people hear what I have to say straight from the horse's mouth." He pointed to a reporter who raised his hand. An aide took the microphone over to him.

"So you're calling yourself a horse?" the reporter asked with a stern expression.

Trumpet smiled, but at the same time he wanted to stake the reporter to an ant hill. "I guess you could call me a work horse, how's that? Now let me get back to what I wanted to say. I will encourage our manufacturers to return to the U.S. Many of them have taken their factories overseas as many of you know."

Another reporter murmured, "Probably because they heard you were going to be President."

A few in the audience chuckled, but Trumpet overheard the remark. Getting red in the face, which was hard to tell because he had spent so much time in the tanning booth, he growled, "Who said that?"

A few reporters looked at the culprit who made the remark, giving him away.

"What's your name?" Trumpet growled, pointing to the guilty reporter.

The man grabbed the microphone from the aide and replied sarcastically, "Brad Pitts."

"You're not Brad Pitts, I've worked with Brad Pitts. You may be Brad Putz but you're not Brad Pitts," Trumpet remarked.

"Yeah, well you're not a real President?" the man shot back, making a face as he said it.

Seeing that this was going nowhere fast, Trumpet motioned for his aide to take the microphone away and made a mental note to have the Secret Service check to see if the man graduated from elementary school. Then gripping the podium tightly, Trumpet explained, "Many of the manufacturers *left* our country because Obahma taxed them into oblivion. This was on his watch, not mine. I plan on lowering the corporate tax rate and doing away with a lot of unnecessary regulations. That will bring them back."

A female reporter raised her hand and took the microphone. "Won't that cause a lot of people in those other countries to lose their jobs? Isn't that extremely callous to put them out of work?"

Trumpet counterpunched. "So if people in our country lose their jobs, that's okay?"

"The people in our country are rich. They can afford to lose their jobs," she brazenly replied.

"Why don't you lose yours then," Trumpet suggested, licking his finger then air drawing a one.

The reporter clenched her teeth tighter than a drum and threw the microphone at him but a secret service agent lunged for it and snatched it in midair. Another agent escorted her out.

Trumpet pointed to the agent who snared the micro-

Chapter 5

phone and said, "How about that Secret Service agent who just saved my life. Let's give him a hand." He began clapping. When he realized he was the only one, he stopped, cleared his throat and said, "Now back to what I plan on doing for our *own* people. I will rebuild our military, defeat ISIS, declare war on the drug cartels, close the border, get rid of criminal aliens in our country, start construction on the Keyrock Pipeline, impose sanctions on countries that have been taking advantage of us and our intellectual property, nominate a justice for the Supreme Court, improve education, stop crime, drain the marsh, blah, blah, blah, blah, blah, blah, blah, blah, blah, blah." He finished with... "and give ice cream cones to every child under ten."

A young boy sitting on a reporter's lap, because she couldn't get a baby sitter, immediately waved his arms and shouted, "I'm four!"

"Get that kid an ice cream cone," Trumpet ordered.

Johnny D., Trumpet's assistant, quickly went out to the smoothie machine in the hall (ordered by Trumpet), and made a chocolate cone with sprinkles. He then took it to the boy and handed it to him.

"He doesn't like sprinkles," his mother said, throwing the cone on the floor.

"But I do like sprinkles," the boy cried, breaking into incessant sobbing.

"Not from him!" his mother uttered, taking him out.

Once the disruption was removed, a reporter from the Washington Compost took the microphone and asked, "What are you going to do about North Korea? Their leader keeps testing missiles and blatantly threatens to use them against us."

"You didn't read my Toot about Rocket Boy, did you?" Trumpet remarked.

"No, what did it say?" the reporter asked.

"Rocket Boy bragged that he had a nuclear button on his desk. I said I had one too, but mine was bigger and it worked," Trumpet replied with a self-assured smile.

The reporter was already thinking of a headline for the next issue of his paper: ***"Trumpet Declares War on North Korea!"***

Jim Acostya from CNN blurted out, "Why do you hate reporters?"

"I don't hate reporters," Trumpet replied. "I just want an honest press that isn't slanted toward one political party or another. Most of you people print and report phony news every day."

Acostya jumped to his feet and pointed at Trumpet. "Aren't you destroying the people's faith in the First Amendment's Freedom of the Press when you call stories phony news? That undermines everyones confidence in the news media. Not all news media outlets are the same, you know!"

Trumpet just smiled and took out a piece of paper from his inside jacket pocket and unfolded it. "All news media outlets aren't the same, you say? Here's a report my staff pulled from the phony news outlets you say aren't the same. ABC reported just today... 'Trumpet is a racist xenophobe.' Here's another from NBC. 'Trumpet is a racist xenophobe.' CBS- 'Trumpet is a racist xenophobe.' Another from MSNBC. 'Trumpet is a racist xenophobe.' And the last one from your outfit. 'Trumpet is a racist xenophobe.' Isn't it interesting that not one of these media outlets have any proof that their claims are correct and they all said the same thing."

"So they just all came to the same conclusion. That's not unusual," Acostya stated.

Chapter 5

Trumpet held out his hands like he was about to bear hug his antagonizer and asked, "Where's the proof?"

"How much money have you got?" Acostya fired back.

"Take the mic from that idiot," Trumpet ordered.

An aide attempted to take the microphone but Acostya pulled it away and said, "You're a rich man. Seriously, how much undeclared money have you received, or should I have your tax returns subpoenaed?"

"You're a reporter. You can't subpoena anything. Now, sit down," Trumpet growled.

"Make me!" Acostya stated defiantly.

Trumpet motioned for his Secret Service guards who pulled out submachine guns and took two steps toward Acostya before he quickly sat down.

Another reporter asked, "What about the reports that people in your campaign contacted the Russian government and its intelligence service?"

"Who are you referring to?" Trumpet asked.

"Paul Manthefort and Carder Page, to name a few," the reporter stated smugly.

"I only had a few people on my campaign staff, but to answer your question, if Carder Page was on my staff, I didn't know him and Paul Manthefort knew some business associates in Ukrane but as far as I know, he had no dealings with the Russians. And despite what the phony news says about Russian ties I might have, I buy all my ties from Sacks 5th Avenue. I wouldn't mind having a better relationship with Russia, but with all the anti-Russian reporting you people have done, that's about as likely as a fly swallowing a potato."

Acostya jumped to his feet again. "So you *would* like to be friends with Pootin! Especially since he helped you win the election."

Trumpet ignored him like he was the invisible man and asked, "Does anyone else have an intelligent question they would like to ask?"

"I've got one," another female reporter shouted. After receiving the microphone, she asked, "One of your *brilliant* executive orders you made instituted a travel ban on several countries with large populations of Islamic people. Any comment?"

Trumpet smiled and said, "Thanks for the compliment. I thought it was a brilliant move as well."

"It wasn't a compliment," the reporter declared, with half-closed eyelids. "Many would consider you a xenophobe for doing that."

Trumpet took in a deep breath and replied, "I instituted the ban to keep Radical Islamic Terrorists from entering our country. Maybe you would like to see another 9-11 but I wouldn't. And why would someone think I'm a xenophobe? Isn't that one of those musical instruments with a bunch of wooden bars you play with mallets?"

The reporter huffed and said, "No, everyone knows its a germ."

Trumpet shrugged and pointed to another reporter.

"Just a follow-up on the last question. The court overturned your travel ban. Why do you think they overturned it?"

"Easy, it was a bad court," Trumpet replied.

"What do you mean it was a bad court?"

"If the judge is an Autocrat, it's a bad court. If he's a Rebubbacan, it's a good court."

"So you think the courts should be political," the reporter stated, with a "gotcha" look in his eyes.

Trumpet gave him a look you'd give a person who

Chapter 5

just announced chickens came from cows and said, "The courts *are* political. The difference is that Rebubbacans believe in following the constitution and Autocrats believe the constitution is more like a set of guidelines you don't really have to follow."

"That's a lie!" the reporter shouted. The Constitution was drawn up by white supremacists and slave owners so it's mostly null and void."

"Where did you get your journalism degree, at the Socialist Secondary School for Oppressed Proletariats?" Trumpet asked.

The reporter displayed a smug smile and replied, "I'll have you know I was first in my class at Karl Marx Kollege in Leningrad."

Trumpet shook his head. "It figures. Next question."

Another reporter took the microphone and asked, "We have a report from the FBI's Director that you fired Mike Flinn for lying. Can you elaborate?"

"I had to fire Mike because he had illicit communications with Russia's U.S. ambassador and lied to the FBI about it." Under his breath he said, "After I told the #%@& director to stop investigating him."

"What kind of illicit communications did he have?" the reporter pressed.

"Evidently he and Russian ambassador Sergey Kissayak discussed sanctions and something about the U.N."

The reporter's eyes expanded to the size of oranges. "Sanctions? You mean killing someone like in the movie, *The Iger Sanction*?"

The reporters in the room gasped.

"No, they discussed penalties. It's complicated and I'd rather not go into it. I was sad to let him go, but I asked H.R. McMasters to replace him, who I think will do a great job. He is a veteran of the Golf War, was a professor at the United States Golf Academy, he's a member of the Council on Foreign Golf Courses, and a Consulting Senior Fellow at the International Institute for Golf Swing Studies"

"What's his handicap?" the reporter asked.

"That's classified," Trumpet stated. "Next question."

Another reporter raised his hand and received the microphone. "Mister President, I understand you had some leaks in the White House recently. Care to comment?"

"We can't have leaks in the White House," Trumpet declared. He turned to his assistant, Johnny D. and said, Johnny, get someone to fix those, will you?"

Suure, Boss. You wanna guy from the West Coast so nobody knows his face?" Johnny asked, putting a cigar in his mouth.

"Wait a minute, Johnny." Turning to the reporter, Trumpet asked, "Are we talking pipes?"

"Personnel leaks," the reporter replied.

Johnny took the cigar out of his mouth and said, "Dats what I tought."

Trumpet put up his hand and said, "We'll handle this another way, Johnny."

His assistant just shrugged.

"What leaks did you hear about?" Trumpet asked the reporter.

"We have transcripts of calls you made to Mexico and Australia," the reporter replied.

Trumpet looked like he was going to spit grenades. "I'll get rid of anyone who leaks information without my authorization."

The reporters hurriedly wrote down his comment, "Trumpet says he will personally kill anyone who leaks information."

Chapter 5

That evening, CNN Tonight had Kwis Chromo and Don Leman reporting Trumpet's news conference.

Leman knocked on Chromo's dressing room door and said, "Hey Kwis! We're on in five minutes. What's taking you so long?"

"I'm getting the last of my makeup done then I have to do a few dumbbell curls. Save my place."

"Yeah, I'll save your place, you privileged brother of a white supremacist sex fiend," Leman mumbled as he walked away.

When Chromo finally arrived at the set, he took his seat and smiled at Leman.

"What the #@%& is on your face?" Leman asked, looking like he was watching someone swallow a worm.

"It's my new makeup," Chromo replied. "It's called Chromium Desire. I also put it on my fingernails."

"You look like an android," Leman remarked, still shocked at his appearance.

"I wanted to impress the viewers with my new look," Chromo responded.

"They won't be impressed when the lights hit your face and all the people see is glare," Leman commented.

Chromo smirked and said, "You may be right, I may be crazy. But it just might be a lunatic they're looking for." He smiled and said, "That was a line from an old Billy Jole tune."

"You'll be singing a different tune if you don't wash that crap off," Leman commented.

"Do you think I have time?" Chromo asked.

Just then, the cameraman blurted, "You're on in five, four, three, two, one..."

"Nope," Leman said as the camera light went on.

"Good evening, I'm Don Leman and the man next to me, who looks like a chromed gear shift knob, is Kwis Chromo. We have breaking news from Trumpet's first press conference. What did the President have to say at his first meeting with the press, Kwis?"

"Well, Don, the most shocking thing was that Trumpet threatened to have whoever leaked his White House telephone calls taken care of, and we know what that means."

A banner underneath their videos read: "Trumpet Orders Mob Hit on White House Leakers."

The same exact banner was flashed across the screen at CBS, MSNBC, ABC, NBC, NPR, and ESPN.

"Yes, we do, Kwis. It's shocking to have our 'so called' President act in such a despicable manner. The Department of Injustice should look into that right away."

"And while they're at it, they should also look into the personal sex lives of his son, his son-in-law, his ex-wife, his daughter, and his daughter-in-law and shoot us a copy of the report," Chromo added.

Leman Puckered. "Why would you want the Department of Injustice to do that?"

Chromo smiled lecherously and replied, "Because I'm a kinky guy."

The next day's front page headline of the Washington Compost read: ***"Trumpet Puts Out Contract on White House Leakers!"***

The front page headline of the New York Grimes read: ***"Trumpet Orders Mafia Assassin to Kill Leakers!"*** The subhead read: ***"Trumpet Also Believed to Be Responsible For Jimmy Huffa Disappearance."***

Chapter Six
It's Muller Time!

It didn't take Trumpet long to discover that none of his campaign promises were going to be honored by the House or the Senate. The only recourse he had was to create executive orders to implement them. The Autocrats went crazy and knew they had to get rid of Trumpet quick before he ruined all their political gains.

FBI Director Comby had made it a habit to keep memos of all his conversations with Trumpet in the event that he would be involved in a trial against the President. He was preparing for the investigation that the Autocratic party was about to launch into Trumpet's alleged involvement with the Russians to affect the country's Presidential election. Comby, however, went one step further. He leaked his memos to a professor at Columbus Law School which was then published in the New York Grimes. The headline read: ***"FBI Director Verifies Trumpet Doesn't Know What a Locus Standi Is."*** Comby added in the article that Trumpet thought it meant where "locusts stood."

When Trumpet found out Comby had leaked the information, his retribution was swift and terrible according to a press briefing by Sean Spicey. He told the reporters that when Trumpet found out there was another leak, he released his Mongolian hordes on central Asia. Later, he had to correct his statement saying that he got his information mixed up with another leader he was reading a book on.

Trumpet fired Comby without resorting to Mongolian hordes, on the recommendations of Deputy Attorney General Rodney Rotenstein. Attorney General Jeff Sayshuns had to recuse himself since he and Comby were both eagle scouts.

With their chief Presidential spy out of commission, over 130 Autocratic lawmakers called for a special counsel to investigate Trumpet's participation in the Russian election interference. Forty Rebubbacan lawmakers expressed questions or concerns like, "Why are individual socks the only things that get lost in the wash?" and "How come every time you drop a cupcake on the floor it always lands icing side down?"

The New York Grimes reported that FBI counter-unintelligence grew concerned about Trumpet's ties to Russia during the campaign but held off opening an investigation because they didn't have any proof. That's why they had to invent some. The FBI combined that counter-unintelligence investigation with a criminal obstruction of justice investigation related to Comby's firing, and came up with a counter-justice-unintelligence-obstruction charge. Attorney General Sayshuns also recused

Chapter 6

himself from that investigation because he was confused, so Deputy Attorney General Rotenstein took over and appointed Robert Muller, a former FBI Director, as Special Counsel. Muller began the investigation, once he figured out what he was investigating.

The reason Rotenstein decided to put a Special Counsel in charge of the probe rather than the FBI was because he was afraid McCave might shoot the witnesses during the investigation if he didn't like their testimonies. Muller was consequently given ultimate power to investigate Russian interference in the elections, including any links between Trumpet's Presidential campaign and the Russian government, any matters that arose from the investigation, and anything having to do with large storms. Consequently, Muller took over the FBI's investigation *Crossfire Tornado* which included Steel's dossier.

Once the Muller investigation officially began, Rottenstein empaneled a grand jury and issued subpoenas to almost every Rebubbacan, Russian, and weatherman he could think of.

A Russian-born lobbyist who met with Donald Trumpet Jr. before the election, was one of the first called to testify in front of the grand jury.

The prosecutor approached him and asked: "Mr. Akmet(mumbles), is it true you met with Donald Trumpet Jr.?"

"Da... yes."

"And what did you discuss in this meeting?"

"I vanted to become distributor for hees seester's clothing line in Moskva. I figured he could introduce me."

"You vanted to become distributor for hees seester's clothing line," the prosecutor mimicked.

"Da, I mean yes. You have good Russian accent."

The prosecutor closed his eyes half way, then said, "Come now, Mr. Akmet... whatever the rest of your name is, do you expect us to believe you wanted to distribute clothes for Ivanka Trumpet?"

"Da."

"And did you give any money to the Trumpets to become a distributor?"

"Da. But I got discount so I could mark up."

"Are you sure this money went to purchase clothing or did it go toward Donald Trumpet's campaign?" the prosecutor asked with eyes blazing, until a juror put them out with a fire extinguisher.

The Russian shrugged his shoulders and replied, "They could do vith money vhatever they vanted. All I vanted vas distribution rights."

"Distribution rights?"

"Da."

"To sell clothing."

"Da."

The prosecutor approached and came face to face with the Russian. "Did Mr. Trumpet Jr. have you sign a contract to distribute his sister's clothing line?" he paused for a second then said, "No, don't tell me. Your Siberian tiger ate it." He walked away with a smug smile on his face as a few members of the jury chuckled.

"Da, I signed contract," the Russian replied. Reaching into his pocket, he pulled out some papers and said, "Here is contract."

The prosecutor walked back to him and snatched the forms from his grasp and perused them. After he finished, he shoved them back to the Russian and said, "There was another Russian with you, wasn't there?"

"Da."

Chapter 6

"And who was that person?" the prosecutor asked, looking at the Russian with a magnifying glass.

"Her name is Natalia Vesnitsky. She is Russian attorney."

The prosecutor's eyebrows raised like shades that had been pulled up quickly. He then squinted and asked, "What was this Russian attorney's reason for being in the meeting?"

"She was there to verify contract but she also mentioned she had documents showing the flow of unlawful funds to Autocratic National Committee and vanted to know if Trumpet Jr. vas interested."

The prosecutor put one finger in the air and said, "Aha! And what did Donald Trumpet Jr. say?"

"He said dat vas hees father's business, not hees."

"And did these unlawful funds that went into the Autocratic National Committee come from Donald Trumpet's campaign fund?"

The Russian looked at the prosecutor like his head was a cantaloupe and replied, "Vhy vould Trumpet give money to Clinkton campaign?"

The prosecutor looked out under his eyebrows and said, "Uh, we'll take a short recess, I need a smoke."

Later, George Papacropolis was also subpoenaed.

"Mr. Papacropolis," the prosecutor began, "Uh, Mr. Papacropolis?" the prosecutor repeated, looking around.

"I'm down here," the 4'11" defendant said.

The prosecutor peered over the solid witness stand railing and said, "Oh, there you are. Mr. Papacropolis. Looks like you need a booster seat. Bailiff! Get this child, er, man a booster seat!"

A middle-aged bailiff ran out of the room and returned shortly with two big couch cushions.

"I couldn't find a booster seat, but I brought these couch cushions," the bailiff reported.

The prosecutor grabbed them and said, "These will have to do." He handed them to Papacropolis and waited for him to arrange them so his head was now visible over the railing. "Now, ahem... do you know a Russian businessman by the name of Sergey Millan?"

"Yes, he has a string of goat farms in Russia I've invested in. Goat milk happens to be a staple of the Russian diet, you know."

"I'm sure it is," the prosecutor responded. "Aren't these goat farms really a cover for the GRU?"

"What's the GRU?" Papacropolis asked.

"It's the main Russian Intelligence Directorate that is responsible for hacking into our computer systems and altering our voting results. You didn't know that?"

"All I know is that he sends me samples of goat milk every month and I feed them to my girlfriend's cat."

The prosecutor made a sour face and mumbled, "So you're a cat person."

"My girlfriend is," Papacropolis corrected him.

The prosecutor stood there for a moment, trying to decide whether to challenge Papacropolis to a ping pong match or move on. He decided to move on.

"Mr. Papacropolis. Did you meet with an Australian diplomat by the name of Alex Downunder at the Queen's English Tavern?"

"Yes."

The prosecutor then leaned down close to Papacropolis and gave him a menacing stare. "And what did you two talk about?"

"The dreary weather in London, mainly."

The prosecutor turned and locked his eyes on a man

Chapter 6

in the jury. "Isn't it true that you also told Mr. Downunder that you were aware of some Russian-hacked emails that belonged to Hillery Clinkton?"

The juror pointed to himself, causing the prosecutor to shake his head.

"Uh, yes," Papacropolis replied.

The prosecutor then whipped around as if being startled by a car backfiring and asked, "And what did you plan to do with those emails?"

"Nothing. I didn't have them, the Russians did. I received a call from a some guy who told me they had emails off of Clinkton's private server and if the Trumpet campaign wanted to use them to discredit her, it would cost 5 million dollars. He even emailed me some samples to verify."

"Did you verify them?"

"I guess. They sounded like something Clinkton would send, but I knew Mr. Trumpet wouldn't spend the money to purchase them."

"Why not?"

"They were recipes, some government stuff, and a few dirty jokes. I didn't think he would be interested."

"Why didn't you inform the Clinkton campaign that the Russians had hacked into her emails?"

"Duh... because she was running against Mr. Trumpet for the presidency. Why would I want to help her?"

"Well, Mr. Papacropolis, because it was the right thing to do. When the FBI questioned you about your contact with the Russian who offered you these emails, you informed them that you hadn't talked to any Russians. Wasn't that a lie?"

"I didn't know the man who called me was a Russian. He could have been an Eskimo for all I knew."

"Mr. Papacropolis, that excuse holds about as much water as a boat made out of screen doors. I'm going to recommend you be charged with lying to the FBI."

Papacropolis shook his head and wished he had a Redd Bull energy drink.

****

Michael Coen, Trumpet's personal attorney, was next to feel the wrath of the Russia investigation. He was called into the Senate Unintelligence Committee to answer questions regarding some alleged violations of campaign finance laws.

Richard Brrrr, the Rebubbacan chairman of the committee, began the inquiry by having Coen state his name and relationship with the President. He then asked Coen if he had any knowledge of campaign finance violations to which Coen replied, "Nope."

"Well, that's good enough for me. I'll turn the questioning over to my distinguished Autocratic Vice Chairman, Mark Worner."

Worner began to foam at the mouth, caused by some left-over toothpaste he didn't completely rinse out that morning. After wiping it off, he held up some papers in front of his face then peered over them so all Coen could see were his piercing eyes. He then raised the papers so his eyes were covered, then he lowered the papers again to reveal his menacing stare. He repeated this a few times until he was sure Coen was sufficiently intimidated. Then he spoke with a voice like Thor. "Mr. Coen. I have two checks in my possession issued to Stormy Weathers, a well-known stripper and porn actress from the account of Donald Trumpet, signed by yourself. I assume this was hush money to keep her from letting the public know that Trumpet is a lecherous, adulterous Lothario. Since

Chapter 6

these checks were issued during the campaign of Donald Trumpet for President, I hereby state for the record that this is a blatant violation of the campaign finance laws. What do you have to say for yourself, Mr. Coen?"

"May I see the checks?

Worner put the enlarged checks up on a video screen and pointed to them with a laser pen that accidentally burned a hole in the screen.

"Oops," Worner said, throwing a cup of water on the hole before it got any bigger. "Anyway, you can see the signatures on the bottom of the checks are yours, Mr. Coen."

"Ah, these checks were drawn from Mr. Trumpet's personal account and not his campaign account and the checks were written to Miss Weathers for, uh, babysitting Trumpet's son, Barren, while Mr. and Mrs. Trumpet were on a date." Coen then gave Worner a wide-eyed look a dog would have that just peed on a Carastan carpet.

Worner grinned like he'd just won the lottery and said, "We've interviewed Miss Weathers, quite a while I might say, ahem, and she told us the money was for sexual favors she performed for Mr. Trumpet. Nothing was mentioned about babysitting, Mr. Coen. How do you explain that?"

Coen looked amazed. "Who are you going to believe? A sleazy porn star or a well-respected attorney?"

Without hesitation, all the Autocratic members of the committee replied, "The sleazy porn star!"

Worner leaned back in his chair, and with an expression mimicking Jaba the Hut, he said, "Looks like you just lied to the committee, Mr. Coen. You're going to jail, ho, ho, ho."

****

The Muller Investigation continued. Streter Pzok, Leesa Page and 12 other Autocratic attorneys who donated to Hillery's campaign were part of the completely unbiased investigative team.

The Muller appointed grand jury called Carder Page next. The prosecutor was sick, so Adam Shifty happily filled in for him.

"Mr. Page. Records show that you took a trip to Russia while you were working for the Trumpet campaign. Was the purpose of your trip to solicit Russian assistance for Trumpet in our election?"

"No, I was invited by university officials to speak on various energy resources. The invitation I received came long before I joined the Trumpet campaign. I even notified Cory Looseandrowsy, who said it was okay as long as I went as a private citizen and not a member of the Trumpet campaign. After the lecture I met some Russian academics and Russian Deputy Prime Minister Arcade Dorkovich."

"AHA!" Shifty shouted, jumping to his feet and pointing toward Page in a dramatic pose. "And what did you talk to Dorkovich about, pray tell?

"He asked me if I had any stock tips and I told him I didn't."

"Come now, Mr. Page. You worked for Merril Linch and you don't have any stock tips? You expect us to believe that?"

The tall, lanky young man smiled and replied, "Giving out stock tips in my position is against the law."

Shifty made a snarly face and sat back down. After flipping through some pages in his notes, he exclaimed, "AHA! Mr. Page, is it true that in January of 2013, you met a man named Victor Potocoffee at an event on ener-

Chapter 6

gy development in China?"

"Yes."

"And isn't it true he happens to be a junior attaché for the Russian consulate in New York?"

"Yes."

"And did you also meet with the same man for drinks in March of that same year?"

Page ran his hand over his bald head and replied, "Yes."

"And why did you meet with Mr. Potocoffee again, may I ask?"

"You may," Page replied, causing Shifty to make a face at him. "I wanted to learn more about the Russian culture and practice my Russian language skills."

Shifty threw himself back in his chair and gave Page a steely look. "M-i-s-t-e-r P-a-g-e," he said slowly for effect. He then lurched forward and, with condemning eyes, shrieked, "Do you really expect me to believe you met with this Russian agent to practice your Russian? Or, was it really to exchange secrets from our government with him?"

"I don't know any secrets. I don't have access to any of those. We just talked about energy."

"HA! Energy? Like how to destroy America's power grid? Like how to blow up America's nuclear reactors? Like how to blot out the sun with giant dirigibles so our solar panels don't work?"

"Actually, we talked about what brand of flashlight batteries worked the best," Page replied.

"Oh, and what brands did you discuss?"

"N-ergizer, Durablecell, and Rayohvac," Page stated.

Shifty gave Page a condemning stare and said, "You know what I think, Mr. Page?"

"I'm afraid to ask," Page mumbled, turning away from the microphone.

"What was that?" Shifty growled.

"I said, I'd love to know what you think."

A Krafty cheesy smile dripped across Shifty's face as he leaned forward and smugly stated, "I think you two worked up a scheme for the Russians to interfere with our election so Trumpet could win. That's what I think. What do you think about what I think, er, thunk, er, thought?"

Page's response was immediate and emasculating. "I wasn't working for the Trumpet campaign then and hadn't even met Mr. Trumpet."

A member of the jury guffawed, then slunk down in his seat.

Shifty leered at him then slowly rose up from his chair like lava about to erupt from a volcano. Page could

Chapter 6

actually see steam rising from his head. Pointing a gavel at Page that Shifty had "borrowed" from Judge Wopner, he glared at him, mostly caused by the bald spot on his head, and stated, "Let it be noted that the witness is being evasive and causing a disturbance! I declare him in contempt and sentence him to 50 years of hard labor!" Shifty then banged the gavel hard on his thumb and yelled, "Son of a borscht-eating Commie pinko!" shaking his throbbing digit in the air as if it would decrease the pain. He then blew on it and made a wish.

After he was reminded by the court recorder that he could only make recommendations to Muller, he dismissed the contempt charge then dismissed Page after four hours of questioning.

Bolting from his chair, Page ran to the bathroom holding his crotch. His ordeal wasn't over yet, however. Streter Pzok would get a FISA warrant from a judge friend of his named Rudy Cazudy to spy on Page's every move and phone conversations. A typical call that the FBI wiretapped went like this:

"Hi, Carder, it's your mother again."

"Hi, Mom. You've got to stop calling me. It's only been ten minutes since your last call. I'm beginning to think you have dementia."

"Oh, no, silly boy. I had that last year... or was it the year before? It doesn't matter. So, what have you been doing since I last called?"

"Well, I clipped my toenails, ate some carrot sticks, and watched ten minutes of The Simpsins."

"Carrot sticks! You should eat food that will help you gain some weight. I'm going to bring you over a big dish of lasagna, lots of French bread, and a triple layer cheesecake I made. I've got to put some meat on your bones or you'll never attract a girl. You know what they say?"

"What do they say, Ma?"

"If the boy is skin and bones, the girl won't take him to her house."

"Isn't that last line supposed to go, 'the girl won't take him home?'"

"Maybe, but the point is... so, what have you been doing since I last called?"

The two FBI agents listening on the other end each gave out blood-curdling screams and quickly erased the recording.

****

Subpoenas came crashing down on other witnesses like a tidal wave. Jason Baloney-spokesman for Paul Manthefort; Sam Clover-co-chair of Trumpet's Presidential campaign; George Nedar-adviser to the UAE crown prince; executives from six public relations firms who worked with the Trumpet campaign; Roger Rock-campaign advisor to Trumpet: Kristine Davis-(known as the Manhattan Mama) who worked for Roger Rock; Randy Crudico-Roger Rock's backchannel to Julian Assahnge of Weakyliks, and Jerome Corset-former Washington bureau chief of Infowarts. Steve Cannon was also subpoenaed but made a deal with Muller to be interviewed by Muller's team rather than the grand jury. Streter Pzok conducted his interview with Leesa Page and another agent present for security and it took place at FBI headquarters.

Cannon was escorted into a room by a large agent who snarled, "Have a seat. Your interrogators will be with you shortly."

The sixty-four-year-old political strategist with flowing gray hair and a round face sat down and looked around at the same 10' x 12' room that Flinn had been

Chapter 6

interrogated in.

After an hour, Pzok and Page entered the room and sat down across from Cannon. Pzok opened a large binder of notes and documents, pulling out one document in particular.

"I have to go to the bathroom," Cannon stated, scrunching his face like an accordion.

Pzok pointed to a wastebasket in the corner.

Cannon looked at Page, who smiled, then he said, "Never mind."

Pzok began the interview: "Mr. Cannon, I have your resignation here where in it you state that Donald Trumpet Jr. committed treason. Just how did Junior commit treason, Mr. Cannon?"

Cannon shook his head and replied, "No, you're twisting my words, you wife-cheating gigolo!"

"Objection! Witness is speculating!" Page shouted, standing up.

"Sustained! Keep your responses to just answering the question without any accusations that may or may not be true, Mr. Cannon," Pzok warned.

"I thought this was an interview, not a trial," Cannon remarked.

"This is whatever I say it is, so just answer the questions," Pzok replied, giving Cannon a wide-eyed stare.

Cannon then went into a Zen meditation ritual for a few seconds, mumbling what sounded like a dog growling, then said, "If you had read my statement carefully, you would have seen that I said Donald Trumpet Junior's meeting with Russians was about as treasonous as tourists wanting to visit Russia."

"Objection! The witness is speculating again," Page shouted.

"Sustained!" Pzok turned to Page and said, "I would say that Junior's meeting with the Russians at Trumpet Tower was a treasonous act, wouldn't you, Leesa?"

Page gave Cannon a diabolical grin and exclaimed, "Absofreakinlutely!"

"Then if that act was treasonous, it stands to reason that you just lied to us," Pzok deduced.

Cannon looked at Pzok like he wanted to cut his head off with a chain saw.

Noticing Cannon's death stare, Pzok scooted his chair back a little. "Now, let's get back to the matter at hand, Mr. Cannon. I have it from a reliable source..."

"CNN," Page blurted out.

Pzok gave her a deprecating glance and said, "Never mind where the source came from, the information I received is that in Junior's meeting with the Russians, they talked about how to destroy Hillery Clinkton's bid for President by giving Junior emails the Russians had obtained plus a compromising photo of Clinkton kissing a goat at a Ukranian petting zoo when she visited Bunter Hiden."

Cannon replied through clenched teeth. "I don't know anything about emails or compromising photos, you'd have to ask Donald Trumpet Jr. about that."

Pzok gave him a smug look and said, "Oh, we plan to, Mr. Cannon. Sooner or later those emails and photos will turn up and when they do..."

"Hello federal penitentiary," Page said with a confident grin.

"I have nothing more to say to you cretins," Cannon remarked.

"Then apparently, you are of no further use to us, Mr. Cannon," Pzok declared. He walked over to the agent

Chapter 6

by the door and whispered, "Agent Kong, escort Mr. Cannon outside, preferably to the middle of the street where he might accidentally get hit by a car."

The agent nodded, struck his chest and grunted.

****

When Muller found out that Pzok had ordered Cannon to be escorted out into the street during rush hour, he removed him and Page from the special counsel team. Pzok immediately texted Page.

"Did Muller call you into his office?" *Streter*

"Yes, and he said we're off the team but didn't give me a reason. What did he say to you?" *Leesa*

"He told me it was because I told Kong to throw him into rush hour traffic after the interview. Kong must have snitched." *Streter*

"That's ridiculous! The traffic wasn't even moving." *Leesa*

"I know! It's just not right. We should be interviewing all these Trumpet miscreants and throwing the book at them." *Streter*

"Which book?" *Leesa*

"It's just an expression, but the Oxford English Dictionary would be my choice." *Streter*

"I have a few law books we could throw at them too." *Leesa*

"I'm afraid it's a moot point now." *Streter*

"Isn't 'moot' what a cow with a speech impediment says?" *Leesa*

"You're a crack-up, girl." *Streter*

****

Trumpet sat at his desk and noticed his phone receiver was slightly off the cradle. He started to pick it up when he heard a voice coming from it that said, "Don't worry, Trumpet has no idea we wiretapped his phone. The man is an imbecile."

Trumpet carefully put the receiver back in its place then turned and punched an inflatable punching bag that looked like a giant hot dog he had behind his desk. The hand-drawn face on it slightly resembled Nancy Lugosi. "This calls for an additional Toot," he uttered.

Trumpet Toot: Just found out today that my phone is tapped in the oval office. I even heard voices on the line admitting it.

Headline in the New York Grimes the next day: ***Trumpet Has Delusions of Demons in His Phone and Hears Voices.***

Chapter Seven
You're Fired!

Trumpet managed to eventually get a few of his senior staff cabinet choices approved by the senate, even though the Autocrats tried to stall the approvals as long as possible. It was no secret that they intended to impeach Trumpet as soon as they could get enough evidence of wrongdoing, even if they had to produce it themselves.

Maxcine Wahwahs and Eric Swallowell went on MSNBC and were asked by Chuck "Tater" Tott if the rumors were true that the Autocratic Party was looking to impeach Trumpet.

"Oh yeah," Swallowell replied unhesitatingly. "We're gonna send that piece of meat back to the hamburger factory as soon as possible."

"What are your feelings, Congresswoman Wahwahs?" Tott asked, trying to smooth more hair over his forehead.

"Impeach, impeach, impeach, impeach, impeach, impeach, impeach!" Wahwahs replied.

"Well, I guess the cat's out of the bag, folks," Tott stated with raised eyebrows.

"I hope not," Swallowell commented. "I'm allergic to cats."

"It's... just an expression," Tott said, with a condescending look.

"I... knew that," Swallowell stated, looking like a circus clown whose pants just fell down. "I was just trying to add some humor." He then broke wind and, with an exaggerated grin, said, "How's that for breaking news, Chuck?"

Joyless Reed, who sat at the desk with Tott, put her

head in her hand, while a stone-faced Tott said, "Yes, thank you for your contributions, Congress-uh, people."

After Swallowell and Wahwahs went off the air, Reed turned to Tott and said, "You know, Chuck, it's really depressing that we now have a President that has no political experience, makes fun of women, threatens reporters and Muslims, and eats hamburgers. We're in a sad place today."

With a sorrowful look, Tott said, "Yes, Joyless, we *are* in a sad place. But things could be worse. We could be working for Foxy News that spreads disinformation to all its viewers."

Reed gave him a look like he had just revealed her social security number over the air. "No, Chuck, I meant our country is in a sad place, not this station."

"Oh," Tott quietly remarked. He looked around, hoping the station manager didn't hear his comment, and tried to smooth more hair over his eyes.

****

At Foxy News, Bill Hammer and Martha McCallem were discussing the days events on America's Homeroom.

"And that's our list of staff birthdays here at the station. Happy Birthday to one and all," Hammer announced, Tooting a noisemaker after his report. "Do you have any announcements, Martha?" he asked.

"Yes, Bill. I was just informed on that little thing in my ear that lets us know when there's breaking news so we can..."

Hammer interrupted. "Yes, Martha, I know what it does, just..."

McCallem interrupted him and said, "Anyway, the Autocrats intend to impeach President Trumpet at their earliest convenience. The speaker..."

Chapter 7

"Rea-ea-ea-ea-ealy," Hammer interrupted again, sounding like Jim Carry in the movie Ace Venture Pet Defective. "What is..."

"Yes, Bill, and it sounds like all the executive orders Trumpet drafted to help the country has really made them mad. So they..."

"But if they will help the country, why are the Autocrats mad?" Hammer asked, looking as bewildered as an Autocrat who accidentally attended a Trumpet rally.

McCallem gave him a critical side glance and replied, "I just happen to have Senator John Kinadee, who's standing by to give us a comment. Senator Kinadee, can you hear me?"

Kinadee came on the screen next to Martha's image and said, "Of course I can hear you. I may be old but I'm not deaf," the senator responded in his backwoods accent.

"Just checking," McCallem stated with a nervous giggle. "So what do you think about the Autocrats wanting to impeach the President, Senator?"

Kinadee snorted like a bull and said, "It's a disgrace! A pure disgrace! The man hasn't been in office a month and they want to get rid of him. It's like, 'Oh no! There's a Rebubbacan pest in the White House! Call out the exterminator!' Here the President is trying to introduce some things that will ease the burden on the American people and the Autocrats are against everything he's trying to do. They've got about as much common sense as a rock. In fact, the rock has more common sense than they do."

Martha laughed and said, "You seem to have a good sense..."

"...of humor," Bill finished her sentence, receiving a look a wife would give her husband who said she was getting fat. "Thanks for your insight on this breaking..."

"...news, Senator," Martha interrupted her broadcast associate, giving him a "Now we're even," look.

"Always happy to comment and get paid for it," Kinadee mentioned with a country grin. "Now you two kiss and make up."

****

Autocratic animosity toward Trumpet continued.

Swallowell went back on MSNBC and suggested that the Autocrats wait until after the midterm elections when they would have a majority in the house before they should impeach Trumpet. He also proudly showed a badge pinned on his shirt that said, "I Voted for Late Term Abortion."

Maxcine Wahwahs had her 80th birthday and 50th face lift. Her birthday wish was to have Trumpet skinned and hung on a meat hook, which was something a person who lured children to her cottage in the woods then ate them would say. Oddly enough, Wahwahs did have a cottage in the woods.

The Autocrats couldn't criticize Trumpet for the programs he had instituted, since they seemed to be working well for the people and made the previous Autocratic administrations look bad. But they could call him a racist, xenophobe, misogynist, homophobe, transphobe, and puppy hater.

Nancy Lugosi called a religious leader she knew, namely Al Sharptone, to declare a holy war against Trumpet and pray that his soul would go to a series of critical racist theory lectures given by Ibram X. Kandi, which was the same thing as being sent to hell.

Even Rebubbacans had called for Trumpet's impeachment. Florida representative, Carlos Curblow contacted Ma Jones magazine and wanted credit for being

Chapter 7

the first Rebubbacan congressman to call for Trumpet's impeachment. He received a free subscription.

George Wil, who was a columnist for the Washington Compost, quit the Rebubbacan Party after Trumpet was nominated and urged Rebubbacans to vote for Autocrats in the midterm elections. The headline in his article read: ***"Trumpet's Policies Discriminate Against Every Color Under The Rainbow!"*** He also promised to send every Rebubbacan that did vote against Trumpet, a cd of Katelin Jenner singing *Somewhere Over the Rainbow*.

Bureaucrats belonging to the Autocratic party sabotaged Trumpet's agenda at every turn and would hold up amendments, refuse orders, and leave legislation that Trumpet supported on their desks until someone noticed. And the unauthorized leaks coming out of the White House continued.

Fed up with the continuous leaks, Anthony Scaramouche, Director of Communications, posted a Toot on Tooter. "Whoever leaked my financial disclosure info which is a felony is in BIG TROUBLE!!!!! I will be contacting @FBI and the @InjusticeDept and @Prince45."

When Riebus read the Toot and saw his tag "@Prince45," he printed it out and marched into Scaramouche's office. Going ballistic, he folded it into a paper airplane and sailed it onto Scaramouche's desk. "How come you tagged me about this Toot of yours, Tony?" he grumbled, like one of the dwarfs in *The Hobitt*. "Are you insinuating that I had something to do with the leaks in the White House? And I'm not talking faucets here."

Scaramouche put his hands out to the side and changed his shocked expression to, "I'm just a poor little innocent lamb," expression. He then laughed and said, "Oh, I must have tagged you by mistake."

At that moment, Trumpet walked in and said, "You two look like you're at odds over something. What's going on?"

Scaramouche smiled and said, "Oh, Prince here thinks I accused him of being responsible for the leak of my financial disclosure and was upset because I tagged him."

Trumpet put on his grumpy face and said, "How many times have I told you guys not to play schoolyard games in the White House? That's it, you're both fired."

"No, I tagged Riebus on a Toot and he overreacted and flew a plane at me," Scaramouche explained.

"Okay, then just Riebus is fired for attempted murder," Trumpet declared.

"But, Chief, it was a paper airplane," Riebus pleaded.

"I warned you to stop calling me 'Chief' so you're fired for that!" Trumpet growled.

"But...but..." Riebus stammered.

Trumpet turned purple. "Are you calling me a 'Butt'?"

"No! No!" Riebus responded, groveling like a kid trying to convince his dad not to spank him.

"You're finished! Get out!" Trumpet shouted.

Dejected and disappointed, Riebus went back to his office. After finding a box and packing his scepter, he was hoping to use someday, photos of his wife, two children and pet aardvark, his Starry Wars figurines, a painting of King Otto of Greece, and an espresso machine, he left the White House under FBI escort and went to his clunky old used car, a 1928 Mercedes Benzz. After piling all his belongings in the trunk, he opened the front door and plopped down in the driver's seat, releasing a huge sigh that could be heard a block away. He looked in the rear

Chapter 7

view mirror at his youthful countenance, thanks to a few sessions at his plastic surgeon, and wondered what he was going to do now. He had a solid contact at a law firm in D.C. and was sure he could hire on there. Especially since he was a former Chief of Staff at the White House. He just had to make sure he asked someone else for a letter of recommendation other than Donald Trumpet.

****

Trumpet wasted no time in appointing a new Chief of Staff, retired general John Killy.

After being summoned, Killy marched into the Oval Office and saluted. "John Killy reporting for duty, Sir," he barked, snapping a crisp salute and scratching behind his ear.

"Thanks for coming General," Trumpet greeted him. "I've just fired my Chief of Staff and I'd like you to replace him. What do you say?"

"Will I get my own tank?" Killy asked.

"Yes, and I'll even throw in a .30 caliber machine gun."

"That won't do," Killy replied brazenly. "I'll need a .50 caliber machine gun or its no deal."

Trumpet studied him like he was a political science textbook for a final exam and said, "You drive a hard bargain, General, but I like that. I'm even going to throw in an AR-15."

"Put a grenade launcher on that baby and we have a deal," Killy countered.

Trumpet smiled and said, "You got it. When can you start?"

"As soon as I finish planting some anti-personnel mines in my back yard. We're having a problem with some damn raccoons."

"How long will that take?" Trumpet asked.

"As soon as I blow them all to hell and back," Killy replied, with a disarming smile.

"Very well, report to me after your mission is complete," Trumpet stated.

Both men then stood up and Trumpet offered his hand while Killy saluted. Then Killy offered his hand while Trumpet saluted. Finally, Trumpet just said, "Get out of here, I have more people to fire."

Sean Spicey heard Trumpet was looking for him, word had it for being a lamebrain press secretary, so he put in his resignation before Trumpet could fire him.

Scaramouche was next on the list, but Trumpet gave Killy the honor. Killy had Scaramouche bound and blindfolded against a wall and was about to order a squad of riflemen to fire when Trumpet appeared in the nick of time and said, "Uh, general, apparently you misunderstood me when I said you could fire Scaramouche."

****

Sarah Huckleberry Sanders, the new press secretary, shoved the last bite of gooseberry muffin in her mouth, swallowed without chewing, took a drink of moonshine her cousins had made, then went to the podium for the daily press briefing. "I have a few announcements before we get started. Feeling that too many pieces of confidential information were leaking from the White House, the President has decided to fire Chief of Staff Prince Riebus and replace him with General John Killy. Anthony Scaramouche was also fired."

"Does this mean there won't be any more leaks?" a reporter called out from the group.

"That will remain to be seen," Sanders tactfully stated, "but General Killy has informed the President that if

Chapter 7

he finds anyone else leaking information he will personally run them over with his tank."

"So Trumpet fired Riebus and Scaramouche because he thought they were the source of the leaks?" another reporter asked.

"If he thought they were the sources, General Killy probably would have shot them," Sanders replied. "I have some other announcements so if you would hold any other questions until I've made my remarks, we can finish in time for lunch. The President has announced he will withdraw from the TPP..."

One reporter turned to another and asked, "What's the TPP?"

The other reporter scratched his head and replied, "I think its the Toilet Paper Partnership."

"Great!" the other reporter exclaimed, "Now we'll run out of toilet paper."

Sanders continued. "He has also decided to withhold funding from Sanctuary Cities..."

One female reporter jumped to her feet shouting, "He can't do that? Half of my family came from Mexico illegally and live in San Francisco! How are they going to get free meals, medical care, and schooling?"

Sanders smiled and said, "I guess they'll have to apply for legal entry like every other immigrant is supposed to. What are their names?"

The reporter wagged her finger at Sanders and sat down mumbling a string of Spanish expletives.

"Along with that, the President will end the catch and release program with Mexico..."

Jim Acostya stood up and asked, "Does this mean Mexicans can keep all the fish they catch now?"

Sanders gave him a weary look and replied, "No,

Jim, they can't keep all the fish they catch. This means illegal aliens won't be released in our country any more after they're caught."

"Caught fishing?" Acostya asked.

Sanders let out a frustrated sigh and said, "Sit down, Jim. Now, as I was saying, the President will also withdraw from WHO..."

A reporter turned to the man next to him. "Who's WHO?"

"How would I know who's WHO? She didn't say who WHO is."

The reporter raised his eyebrows then muttered, "We sound like a bunch of owls."

"The President has also announced that he will approve construction on a badly needed wall around our southern border," Sanders continued.

A female Tellemundo reporter immediately shouted, "Trumpet is a racist!" and threw one of the huaraches she was wearing at Sanders.

Sanders caught it in midair and said, "You're a bad shot, Maria."

The reporter took off her remaining huarache and tossed it at Sanders who caught it in her other hand.

Sarah ended the briefing and hurried out with two huaraches and a smug smile saying, "They're mine now."

Sanders, however, later returned them to the Tellemundo reporter in a shoebox with a note that said, "Sorry, for taking your huaraches. I had the President autograph them as a keepsake for you."

After reading the note, Maria took the box of shoes to her recycling bin and threw them in.

****

The Inspector General for the Department of In-

Chapter 7

justice under Trumpet was Michael Horrorwitz. Horrorwitz announced that he would examine evidence related to "allegations of hanky-panky" regarding James Comby's handling of the investigation into Hillery Clinkton's email practices and whether Injustice Department employees improperly leaked information prior to the Presidential election. Consequently, he called Andrew McCave to testify, since McCave was supposedly investigating the Clinkton foundation as acting director of the FBI after Comby's firing.

McCave was sworn in then the questioning began.

Horrorwitz, (taking a bite of a half-eaten sandwich): "Sorry, they called me in here before I finished my lunch. Now, Mr. McCave... chomp, chomp..."

"That's FBI Acting Director, Mr. Horrorwitz," McCave corrected him.

Horrorwitz narrowed his eyes and swallowed: "Mr. McCave, we have information that you leaked the fact you pretended to investigate the Clinkton Foundation to the Journal."

McCave glowered at Horrorwitz and said, "That's a lie! I never leaked any information to the Journal. Where did you get that baloney?"

Horrorwitz looked down at his sandwich and replied, "From the deli down the street... oh, you mean the information. I received it from a recording FBI attorney Leesa Page made."

McCave shook his head and muttered, "That ignorant slut!"

"You just lied under oath, Mr. McCave. I'm recommending that you be fired," Horrorwitz said, as he took another bite of his sandwich.

"FBI ACTING DIRECTOR!" McCave bellowed.

That afternoon, he received an email from Donald Trumpet that said, "Warmest Regards, You're Fired!"

****

Donald Trumpet's chief strategist, Steve Cannon, was the next to feel the axe. A far right rally in Virginia, intended to unite all conservatives, resulted in violence. Both parties condemned the violence but the New York Grimes called Trumpet's official comment that the violence erupted from both sides, insensitive and racist. The headline read: *"Trumpet Responsible for Violence and Hatred at Rally."*

Cannon advised the President to say the violence was caused by both sides. The Washington Compost found out and labeled Cannon a racist and a symbol of white supremacy in their next edition.

The headline read: *"Cannon Says Violence from White Supremacists is Okay!"*

John Killy took the paper and showed it to Trumpet. "Did Cannon say this?" he bellowed.

Trumpet chuckled and said, "I stopped believing the Compost and Grimes a long time ago. Have Cannon come to my office and we'll get his side of the story."

Killy saluted, did an about face and marched out.

A short while later Cannon appeared with Killy and boomed. **"The headline in the Compost is a bald-faced lie, even if the headline had whiskers it's a bald-faced lie!"**

"But you can see how bad this makes us look," Killy stated. "Taking the side of white supremacists is as bad

Chapter 7

as taking the side of those who think the white race is superior to others."

"You just said the same thing, Einstein," Cannon informed him, "and I never said white supremacist violence is okay. I actually condemn it."

"Oh, then why did the headline indicate you thought it was okay?"

"Because the reporters for that rag are a bunch of lying scumbags!" Cannon roared.

"You mean the press *lies* to the American people?" Killy stated, looking like a teenage boy who had just asked a girl to the prom and been turned down.

"That's all they do," Trumpet stated.

"Well, if the inquisition is done here, I'm going back to my office," Cannon growled, storming out.

Killy turned to Trumpet with a stern look and said, "I don't like the insubordinate way he reacted. I think he should be fired or at least do 500 push-ups."

"You handle it, John. I've got a Toot to write about a kid being hammered by the press for wearing one of my hats and smiling at an Indian activist."

"I'll take care of it, Sir."

The next day, Killy asked Cannon to turn in his resignation or do 500 pushups. Cannon chose to fire off a scathing resignation stating that the accusation he approved violence at the rally was about as true as Donald Trumpet Jr. committing treason.

Trumpet Toot: Fired Riebus and McCave. Cannon submitted his resignation. It almost feels like I'm back on The Adventist.

Chapter 8
Random Acts of Nonsense

Before Sarah Huckleberry Sanders conducted another press conference, she drank a tall glass of green tea mixed with some powdered Xanex then took the podium.

The press had all taken their seats and were excited to let the games begin. The best pseudo-journalists sat in the front row gnashing their teeth and making obnoxious hyena sounds.

"You all seem to be in good spirits today," Sanders commented, which drew an evil cackle from the back. "Okay, maybe not *good* spirits," she amended her greeting. "First, a few announcements before I take questions. The President has decided to fire Prince Riebus for calling the President a 'butt,' Andrew McCave was fired for lying to the AG, and Steve Cannon resigned rather than do 500 pushups. I'll take questions now."

A reporter raised his hand.

"Yes?" Sanders acknowledged him.

Chapter 8

The reporter, looking eerily like a reincarnation of the old Hungarian film actor, Peter Lorry, stood up and said with a thick accent, "Yes, I am Petrof Lorinski of Budapest Beacon and was wondering why McCave was fired for lying. The President lies and no one fires him. Reboobycans lie and no one fires them. Everybody lies and nobody fires them."

A lady sitting next to him tugged on his sleeve and whispered something in his ear.

"Yes, I mean to say everybody lies except press. Don't you thinking that to fire McCave was little harsh? It seems like President thinks he's back on TV show."

Sanders gave him a "You're a doofus" look and said, "Lying to the AG is a violation of the law. McCave was lucky he was fired and not prosecuted."

"Yes," the Hungarian reporter replied, "but it's not really serious violation of law, is it? Isn't it more like, 'Oops, my bad?'"

"Would you like me to recite 18 U.S. code sub section 1038 to you?" Sanders responded.

The reporter sat down and mumbled, "You don't have to get miffy, Trumpet stooge lady."

Jim Acostya raised his hand.

Sanders rolled her eyes like a pair of dice and sighed, "Yes, Jim?"

Acostya stood up and bowed to his peers then raised one eyebrow and asked, "You said Steve Cannon resigned, but I have a source inside the White House kitchen that says Cannon was fired for siding with white supremacists at that far right rally in Virginia that resulted in violence. My source even said he heard Cannon say if he had been there, and I quote, "I would have kicked some liberal butt myself." Since we've established the fact that the President lies and since you're speaking for the President, then you just lied in your opening statement."

"Who was your source in the White House kitchen?" Sanders asked.

"I'm not willing to give up my original source, but let me say the cook's parrot has a reputation for being accurate in only repeating what it has heard."

"The cook's parrot," Sanders chuckled.

"Yes, and it has a great singing voice too," Acostya stated with a haughty expression.

"Is your source an Autocrat or a Rebubbacan?" Sanders asked.

"You give me twenty bucks and I'll tell you," Acostya replied with a cheesy grin.

Sanders sighed again and said, "Sit down, Jim."

****

The T.V. show *"The Slanted View"* decided to spend the bulk of their time one day on Donald Trumpet. The panel was discussing Trumpet's claim on Foxy News that Obahma wiretapped him which most of the panel rejected. The principal of the show, Joi Bayhar stated that Trumpet went on Foxy News because they stoop to his level, meaning Foxy News and Trumpet both lie to the public. A female guest, who had worked at Foxy News, said, "That's not true. When Foxy News reports something in error, they correct it. Do you know how many people watch Foxy News in this country? There's a lot of people who watch it, and there's a lot of people who voted for Donald Trumpet that feel Foxy News represents their view. And they're happy that's represented in the news somewhere because it certainly isn't represented here."

Whoopie Coldburger, a regular on the Slanted View, fired back saying, "Just don't represent Foxy News reporting as facts because all of it is bull and the viewers who believe it are all idiots. Not only that, but Talker Carlson laughs like a baboon."

****

Jeff Sayshuns appointed Matthew Whitacher as Chief of Staff for the Justice Department then recused himself for doing it. A month before Whitacher took the job, he wrote an opinion column for CNN entitled, "Muller's investigation of Trumpet is going too far." He also asserted that the Trumpet Tower meeting between Donald Jr. and the Russians was not improper and there was no evidence of collusion.

He barely managed to get his feet wet in the deluxe foot spa provided by the department, when Trumpet asked for Sayshuns resignation for excessive recusing.

Trumpet appointed Whitacher as acting A.G., who assumed the oversight of the Muller investigation.

The Autocrats and RHINOs were quick to accuse him of having a conflict of interest because of his previous pro-Trumpet statements, and that he should recuse himself from overseeing.

Not wanting to be branded as an excessive recuser like Sayshuns, Whitacher thumbed his nose at them.

MSNBC, however, was not going to let him off that easy. They asked him to come on the Chris Madviews show and defend his position, or in other words, get grilled like a ham and cheese sandwich.

Madviews: "Good evening loyal liberal viewers, tonight I have a special treat for you. No, it's not free weed, we have Matthew Whitacher, Trumpet's confused acting Attorney General on the show tonight. Get ready to play a little kickball where we like to kick our political opponents when they're down. You ready for some kickball acting A.G. Whittacher?"

Whitacher: "Actually, I prefer football, Chris. I was a tight end at..."

Madviews: "I could care less about your athletic accomplishments, Whitacher, I'm more interested in why you didn't recuse yourself from overseeing the Muller investigation."

Whitacher: "Well, Chris, there was no reason..."

Madviews: "And that's the difference between liberals and conservatives. Liberals operate on logic and reason while conservatives admit they have no reason."

Whitacher: "Actually, Chris, I was going to say there was no reason to recuse myself because I was willing to accept Muller's findings without bias or prejudice."

Madviews: "But you already showed your bias by stating, and I quote, 'Muller's investigation of Trumpet is going too far.' Did you or did you not say that?"

Whitacher: "Yes, I said that, but I believe that Muller's investigation should stick to the perameters it was given. Demanding Trumpet's tax returns is not relevant to the accusation that he colluded with the Russians to win the election."

Madviews: "Of course it's relevant. If Trumpet paid the Russians to rig the election, which there is undisputable evidence he did, then it will show up on his tax returns probably as a charitable contribution."

Whitacher: "You have undisputable evidence that Trumpet paid the Russians?"

Madviews: "Well, I personally don't, but Congressman Shifty says he does, and everyone knows he is a paragon of truth, justice, and the Autocratic way."

Whitacher: "I would agree on the Autocratic way, but I would dispute the others."

Chapter 8

Madviews: "That's the problem with you Rebubbacans. You can't recognize truth even when it slaps you upside your head."

Whitacher: "Well, I can certainly recognize the linebackers that slapped me upside my head, and that happened on more than one occasion."

Madviews: "Are we back to football again? Maybe those linebackers slapped you upside your head one too many times so you're a little loopy when it comes to truth and fiction."

Whitacher: "I'm clear on both, Chris. Truth is verity and fiction is fabrication."

Madviews: (in a mocking tone) "Truth is verity and fiction is fabrication. Well, folks, as you can see, our guest is obviously trying to confuse us with his advanced vocabulary. You can email me at Madviews@MSNBC.com and I'll give you the definitions as soon as I can look them up myself. That about wraps it up for this session of kickball. Tune in tomorrow for a special interview with Nancy Lugosi. She's going to explain how she can know what's in a bill without reading it. Don't miss it."

****

Before Trumpet was declared President, Hiden's son, Bunter, had been employed by a natural gas company in the Ukrane called Burrrizma that specialized in capturing cow methane emissions and converting them into natural gas. Bunter said his father had nothing to do with his appointment to the company's board of directors even though Joe was overseeing policy to fight corruption in Ukrane and made the decision as to whether Ukrane received any financial aid from the U.S. When Joe found out that the Ukranian government had launched an investigation into Burrrizma for corruption, he threatened to withhold aid if they didn't fire the prosecutor. Well, whadya know, they caved to Joe! The Ukranian prosecutor was fired, Ukranian cows just kept on emitting those organic vapors and Bunter Hiden kept getting those huge checks from Burrrizma. Shortly afterwards, Obahma called the Ukranian President.

"Hey, Victor, Obahma here."

"Meester President. What do I owe this unexpected surprise?"

"I need a favor, Victor. My lamebrain Vice President's son, Bunter, works for Burrrizma and it would look bad for me if he was charged with anything. Could you do me a favor and drop the investigation?"

"I could do it for say... a few million in gold."

"How about I send you a few million dollars?"

"No, Spasiba. Your dollar is losing its value every day so I would prefer that you make payment in gold."

"You drive a hard bargain, Victor. Naturally, this is our little secret and you won't say anything about it, right?"

"Of course, Meester President. I vouldn't dream of saying anything."

"I knew I could count on you, Victor. That's all I had. Oh, one more thing. Next time you're in D.C., arrange a meeting with Trumpet. When the press is around, shake his hand and say, 'Thanks for the insider trading information.' You got it?"

"But what if he doesn't give insider trading information to me."

"It doesn't matter. Just say it and the press will do the rest."

"As you vish, Buhrockski."

"Great. Goodbye, Victor."

Chapter 8

"Goodby, Meester President."

After Victor Yamakovich hung up the phone, he turned to his aide and said, "If payment to keep quiet about Hiden is ever discovered, you tell press that Obahma paid us. That vay I keep promise not to say anything since you vill be saying. Da?"

"Da," his aide agreed, as his boss broke into a song about cow emissions and stock market trades.

****

Before Trumpet's presidency, Joe Hiden attended the Council on Foreign Relatives to discuss issues of concern. He brought up the meeting he had in Ukrane concerning a loan they requested. When asked about it, this is what Joe said:

"I'm given assignments by the President and one of them was to arrange for a billion dollar loan to that country over by Russia... was it Holland? No, Ukrane. Well, I went over there and it became very obvious to me how corrupt their, uh... what's the guy that prosecutes cases for the state called? Oh, yeah, the state prosecutor. He was investigating, of all things, corruption in a company called, uh... let me see... it rhymes with charisma..."

"Burrrizma," a reporter in the room calls out.

"Yes, thank you, Burrrizma. My son is on the board of that company. It's not a real board like a piece of lumber, it's like the leaders of the company. So, anyway, I knew there couldn't be any corruption on the company's part because my son is on the board. I already explained that it's not really a board, didn't I? Well, since it couldn't be the company, it had to be the state prosecutor. So I called the Ukranean President and said that if he didn't fire the state prosecutor, he wasn't going to get the billion dollars. He told me, uh... what did he tell me? Oh yeah, he told me I didn't have the authority to withhold the funds and only the President could do that. I told him to stuff it, because the President gave me the authority and if he didn't believe it to give him a call. He hummed and hee-hawed for a moment, then I said, I'm leaving here in... uh... six hours and if you haven't fired the prosecutor by then, you aren't getting the billion dollars. Well, son of a (bleep). They fired him. Speak loudly and carry a big board... that's my motto, and I'm talking a wooden board."

"Thank you Mr. Hiden for your, uh, time."

"And thank you, Mr. Chairman, for letting me demonstrate how American diplomacy works."

****

Senators Bernie Slanders and Borey Cooker were walking down the steps coming from the senate chamber where they had just held confirmation hearings on Trumpet's pick for the new attorney general.

Cooker: "What do you think of Trumpet's choice for AG?"

Slanders: "BilBar will just be another yes man for the President and will probably undo all our fabricated investigations into Rebubbacan malfeasance. He shouldn't even be the attorney general. I have it on good authority that when he was working for Bush, he took bribes."

Cooker: "Really? What kind of bribes?"

Slanders: "I heard the Mafia paid off his mortgage and bought him three, no, four brand new cars, and paid for his daughter's college tuition and his golf club membership at MirrorLoggo."

Cooker: "Wo. How come nobody filed charges against him?"

Slanders: "Who wants to go against the mafia? They'll put your dog's head in your bed if you investi-

Chapter 8

gate them then plant crabgrass in your yard while you're asleep. I have enough problems just keeping the damn neighborhood kids off my lawn."

Cooker: "Maybe we shouldn't confirm him then."

Slanders: "It won't do any good. The Rebubbacans have the numbers and they'll just ram him through."

Cooker: "Yeah, you're probably right. So what are you doing for dinner tonight?"

Slanders: "I haven't made any plans yet."

Cooker: "Why don't you come over to my house. I'm frying some chicken, yams, and tarot roots on the barbecue. I have a special sauce that will make your eyes water for days."

Slanders: "Nothing spicy for me, the old ulcer can't handle it. Besides, what are you doing frying chicken? Don't you know white people think that's all you black people eat?"

Cooker: "I don't care what they think. I happen to like chicken."

Slanders: "Well, you really shouldn't feed into their stereotypes if you ask me."

Cooker: "Feed into their stereotypes... good one, Bernie."

Slanders: "What? I don't get it."

****

On Foxy News, Talker Carlson interviewed Michael Avanaughty, who was the attorney for Stormy Weathers in her NDA lawsuit against Donald Trumpet. Carlson affectionately referred to him as the "Creepy Porn Attorney." Avanaughty had been promoting himself on all the liberal news stations as a Presidential candidate before the election and appeared to be thriving while his client was working in a strip club. Carlson wanted to know why she had to work as a stripper after supposedly receiving a large amount of money from the lawsuit settlement. This is the interview:

Carlson: As Stormy Weathers attorney you seem to be doing well wearing $1,000 suits while she's working strip clubs in little towns and wearing next to nothing. You've done tens of millions dollars worth of free media on the basis of your relationship with her and she's working in strip clubs. Why aren't you paying her part of what you're making? You're exploiting her.

Avanaughty: This is absurd. I have not exploited...

Carlson: It's not absurd, those are the facts.

Avanaughty: No, you don't know the facts...

Carlson: Is she working in strip clubs?

Avanaughty: Are you going to continue interrupting me...

Carlson: I do know the facts, actually.

Avanaughty: ...no, you don't because you just demonstrated your ignorance... you didn't even know Michael Coen pleaded to two felonies associated with campaign finance violations.

Carlson: I'm not defending Coen. Why is Stormy Weathers working in seedy strip clubs while you're on TV wearing expensive suits?

Avanaughty: BECAUSE SHE WANTS TO!

Carlson: Oh, she wants to have people throw things at her...

Avanaughty: This is America. If a woman wants to perform in a strip club she...

Carlson: But you're getting richer and she's not.

Avanaughty: I'm not getting richer.

Carlson: Of course you are.

Avanaughty: ...people like you demean her...

Chapter 8

Carlson: I'm not demeaning her. You're the one...

Avanaughty: You're the one that refers to her consistently as a porn star...

Carlson: Right.

Avanaughty: ...and meanwhile you give the President...a pass to have unprotected sex with a porn star...

Carlson: Oh, OK, so now you're calling her a porn star...answer my question. Why are you making money off your client and she's working in seedy strip clubs?

Avanaughty: Sir, do you have any idea how much money I've earned from this case?

Carlson: You were on nearly every cable show when you ran for President and you were paid for that, right?

Avanaughty: You don't even know your facts...how do you have a show and you're this ignorant?

Carlson: Here's what I know for a fact...your client is not thriving. And for you to look me in the eye and say she wants to perform in strip clubs with people throwing stuff at her...insulting her...people don't do that unless they have no choice or she just likes it. Is that what you're saying?

Avanaughty: You don't know anything about my...

Carlson: It's the fact that you're exploiting her.

Avanaughty: ...you don't know anything about my client.

Carlson: I know that she's working in a strip club...

Avanaughty: Can I finish?

Carlson: Please do.

Avanaughty: All right. I've done a remarkable job for my client and she'll be the first one to tell you that. And had you listened to any of her interviews or seen.... any of her comments you would know exactly what she thinks of me. I am not exploiting my client.

The interview continued, but later Avanaughty was

135

convicted of several felonies in an attempted extortion of a sports apparel company. He was also indicted in two states on federal counts including tax evasion, extortion, fraud, and embezzlement. Avanaughty also faced charges of wire fraud, identity theft, and embezzling almost $300,000 from Weathers. Maybe that's why she was working seedy strip clubs.

****

In April, the New York Grimes and Washington Compost were jointly awarded the Pullitzer Prize for their stories on the collusion between Trumpet and the Russians to win the election.

Trumpet Tooted: The New York Grimes and Washington Compost were just awarded the Bullshitzer Prize for phony news reporting. It should have gone to ABC, NBC, CBS, MSNBC, CNN, and NPR too.

Chapter 9
The Proof, the Whole Proof, and Nothing but the Proof

During his confirmation hearings to replace Jeff Sayshuns, BilBar sent a memo to Rodney Rotenstein.

"*Dear Rodney,*

It has come to my attention that Muller's intention to pursue a potential obstruction of justice charge by Trumpet is without merit and has the appearance of a political hatchet job to overthrow the President. Pursue this extremely stupid course of action at your own risk.

Signed
The next AG of the United States
BilBar"

A month later, BilBar *was* the new attorney general and Bob Muller filed the special counsel's final report on the investigation of Trumpet's participation in Russia's meddling of the election. The counsel indicted 34 people, collecting unpaid taxes, seizing assets, and collecting fines. Essentially, Muller investigated anyone who worked for Trumpet's campaign including all their school teachers, friends, business associates, family, and classmates.

The FBI also staged a pre-dawn raid of Roger Rock's residence in Florida and several heavily armed agents took him in custody at gunpoint after making sure there were no uzis hidden in his pajamas. Then they handcuffed the sixty-six-year-old political consultant and hauled him away. Prior to the arrest they notified CNN to make sure they had plenty of video that aired on every news program. One agent who was interviewed by CNN said, "This will send a message to all those white supremicists who side with Trumpet and the Russians that your days are numbered."

Rock was charged for being involved with Weakyliks and discussing Hillery Clinkton's Russian-hacked financial information with some Russian stooge named Curly. He was eventually convicted of lying to Congress about his golf handicap and tampering with witnesses' long playing records by playing them backwards to hear hidden messages.

When BilBar received the special counsel's investigative report, he concluded that the counsel's findings did not establish that the President had committed obstruction of justice, the original charge. The Autocrats, however, were not satisfied with Bilbar's opinion. They took the report to a sympathetic federal judge who ruled that the report should be made public so the people could judge for themselves.

BilBar eventually released the redacted report to the House Judicious Committee after they threatened to charge him with contempt and take away his White House commissary pass. The report indicated that although there was no proof that Trumpet or any member of his campaign had been actively involved with the Russians to affect the election, the Autocrats believed that Trumpet had secretly hoped that the Russians *would* interfere, which was enough to convict him. All the Autocratic attorneys on the special counsel thought Trumpet should be charged with obstruction of justice, but they only had enough statutory evidence to charge him with lying on his golf scores. Muller's report stated that the counsel couldn't prove that Trumpet committed a serious crime but it also couldn't exonerate him. Which meant the ball was in Congress's court. The Autocrats thought that was unfair because the Rebubbacans were taller.

Chapter 9

So, the Autocratic controlled House Judicious and Untelligence Committee quickly subpoenaed Muller to appear before their committee. Their goal was to find something that may have been overlooked in the investigation they could use to impeach Trumpet.

Muller reluctantly appeared.

Jerry Madler: "The Judicious Committee will come to order. Members of the committee will kindly wake up and pay attention to the witness," he said, banging the gavel down hard and giving an indignant glance at several committee members who raised their heads off their desks and rubbed their eyes. "Director Muller, thank you for being here. I'm sure everyone on the committee admires your record of service in the military and our government and I'm sure because of your impeccable record we can rely on your testimony to be accurate and truthful. Over the course of your investigation, blah, blah, blah, blah... You convicted President Trumpet's campaign chairman, his deputy campaign manager, his national security advisor and his personal lawyer, among others... blah, blah, blah... Russia's attacks were designed to benefit the Trumpet campaign... blah, blah, blah... he attempted to prevent witnesses from cooperating with your investigation... blah, blah, blah... you made clear that he is not exonerated... blah, blah, blah... not even the President is above the law. Director Muller, this committee has a responsibility to address the evidence that you have uncovered..." under his breath he stated, "as long as it makes Trumpet look bad," then continued. "You recognize as much when you said, quote, "The Constitution requires a process other than the criminal justice system to formally accuse a sitting President of wrong doing," close quote. That process begins with the work of this committee.

We will act with integrity, we will follow the facts where they lead, we will consider all appropriate remedies including acupuncture, we will destroy every Rebubbacan who voted for Trumpet... strike that last statement... then we will make our recommendation to the House. I have now concluded my opening remarks." Madler stood up and took a bow. Autocratic members of the committee applauded while the Rebubbacan members gargled water. After giving his Rebubbacan colleagues a deprecating glance, Madler sat down and said, "We will now hear from our rank, uh, ranking member, Mr. Callings for his opening statement."

Doug Callings: "Thank you, I think, Mr. Chairman, and thank you Mr. Muller for appearing. And while the report you provided stated that no American conspired with Russia to interfere in our elections, the Autocrats still insist that Trumpet is guilty of that very accusation even though no concrete evidence was obtained."

Madler: "Objection. This hearing has nothing to do with concrete or any other building material and Mr. Callings is speculating."

Callings: "I'm speculating? Okay, then where's your proof the President has broken any law?"

Madler: "I'm sure Mr. Muller will get to that. Are you finished with your opening statement, Mr. Callings?"

Callings: "No, I'm not, Mr. Madler. Now, Director Muller, we were told, collusion was in plain sight even if the special counsel's team didn't find it... blah, blah, blah... burden of proof for accusations that remain unproven is extremely high... blah, blah, blah... no one in the President's campaign colluded... blah, blah, blah... I've read the special counsel's report and here are the facts:. Russia meddled in the election, the President did not conspire

Chapter 9

with the Russians and nothing we hear at this committee today will change those facts... blah, blah, blah... ensure government intelligence and law enforcement powers are never again used and turned on a private citizen or political candidate... blah, blah, blah, blah... ensure our government officials don't weaponize their power against the constitutional rights guaranteed to every U.S. citizen... blah, blah, blah... We've had the truth for months: No American conspired to throw our election. I yield back to the chairman."

Rebubbacan members of the committee applauded and this time the Autocratic members gargled water.

Madler: "Thank you for your version of the truth, Mr. Callings, now I'll turn the time over to Mr. Muller who will give us the proof, the whole proof, and nothing but the proof that the President is guilty. Mr. Muller."

Robert Muller: "Good morning, chairman Madler, the... and rank member Callings..."

Callings: "That's ranking member Callings."

Muller: "Sorry, my hearing isn't as good as it used to be. As you know, I was assigned to serve as special counsel and sort out this mess. I undertook that role because I believe that it was my solemn duty to determine if Russia had interfered in the Presidential election and if the President was involved. Blah, blah, blah, blah... we needed to do our work as thoroughly as possible... blah, blah, blah, blah... decisions were made based on the facts and the law... blah, blah, blah, blah... submitted a confidential report to the attorney general... blah, blah, blah, blah... focused on whether the evidence was sufficient to charge any member of the campaign... blah, blah, blah... Based on Justice Department policy and principles of fairness, we determined we wouldn't decide whether the President committed a crime. Blah, blah, blah, blah... ongoing matters within the Justice Department, and deliberations within our office... blah, blah, blah, blah... conducted an extensive investigation over two years... blah, blah, blah... challenges to our democracy... blah, blah, blah... Russian government's effort to interfere in our election is among the most serious... blah, blah, blah... Russian government greatly interfered in our election... did not establish that members of the Trumpet campaign conspired with the Russian government... didn't make a decision as to whether the President committed a crime... blah, blah, blah... judicial orders limit the disclosure of information... blah, blah, blah... Russian government's effort to interfere in our election is among the most serious and deserves the attention of every American. Thank you, Mr. Chairman."

Madler: "Thank you, Mr. Muller. We will now proceed with questions and I'll start with myself. Director Muller, the President claimed that your report found there was no obstruction and that it completely and totally exonerated him. But your report didn't say that, did it?"

Muller: "That is correct.

Madler: "Does your report say there was no obstruction on the President's part?"

Muller: "No."

Madler: "In fact, you were unable to conclude whether the President committed obstruction of justice or not, isn't that right?"

Muller: "Well, at the outset we... when it came to the President's culpability, we needed to... we needed... we needed to go forward only after taking into account that a President... sitting President cannot be... uh, indicted."

Madler: "So the report didn't indicate that he did *not* commit obstruction of justice, is that correct?"

Chapter 9

Muller: "Yes."

Madler: "And did you actually totally exonerate the President?"

Muller: "No."

Madler: "In fact, your report clearly states that it doesn't exonerate the President. Isn't that correct?"

Muller: "Yes."

Madler: "And you actually found, and I quote, "multiple acts by the President that could have exerted undue influence over law enforcement investigations, including Russian interference and obstruction investigations." Is that correct?"

Muller: "Correct."

Madler: "Now, Director, can you explain in plain terms, so the Rebubbcans can understand, what that finding means?"

Muller: "Well, the finding indicates that the President was not... that the President was not, uh, exculpated for the acts that your party says he allegedly committed."

Madler: "In fact, weren't you talking about incidents, quote, "in which the President sought to use his official power outside of usual channels," unquote, to exert undue influence over your investigations. Is that right?"

Muller: "That's right."

Madler: "So your report also states that President Trumpet's efforts to exert undue influence over your investigation intensified after the President became aware that he personally was being investigated?"

Muller: "Whatever it says in the report."

Madler: "Is it correct that if you concluded that the President committed the crime of obstruction, you couldn't publicly state that in your report or here today?"

Muller: "Well, I would say you could... the statement

would be to... that you would not indict, and you would not indict because a sitting President... burp! Excuse me... cannot be indicted. It would be unconstitutional."

Madler: "But under Department of Justice policy, the President *could* be prosecuted for obstruction of justice after he leaves office, right?"

Muller: "That's true."

Madler: "Did the President refuse a request to be interviewed by you and your team?"

Muller: "Yes."

Madler: "Yes... everyone heard that?" Madler looked around at the Autocrats nodding their heads.

"And is it true that you tried for more than a year to get an interview with the President?"

Muller: "Yes."

Madler: "Yes and yes. And didn't you tell the President's lawyer that an interview with him was vital to your investigation?"

Muller: "Yes."

Madler: "Yes, yes, and yes. But the President still refused."

Muller: "Yes."

Madler: "Ladies and gentlemen, we have four yeses. And did you ask him to submit written answers to your questions?"

Muller: "Yes."

Madler: "Another yes to all the no's the President gave you. Did the President provide any answers to the questions you submitted?"

Muller: "I'm not certain."

Madler: "Okay, thank you Director Muller. Now I'm no legal scholar, but I do believe anyone else who'd engage in the conduct described in your report would

Chapter 9

have been criminally prosecuted because no one is above the law. I now will open the floor for more questions by our committee. You only have 5 minutes, starting with our rank, uh, ranking member, Mr. Callings."

Callings gave Madler a look you would give an opposing cage fighter, then began his questioning.

Callings: "Mr. Muller, I have several questions. Because I only have five minutes, I'll be brief. Since closing the Special Counsel's office, have you conducted any additional interviews or obtained any new information in your role as Special Counsel?"

Muller: "In the... in the... in the wake of the report?"

Callings: "Since the closing of the office."

Muller: "And the question was, have we conducted... uh..."

Callings: "Have you conducted any new interviews, with any new witnesses, anything?"

Muller: "No."

Callings: "At any time in the investigation, was your investigation curtailed or stopped or hindered?"

Muller: "No."

Callings: "In your report you did a lot of work... a lot of subpoenas, a lot of pin registers... so you're very thorough."

Muller: "What?"

Callings: "You're very thorough."

Muller: "Oh, I thought you said, 'You're a hairy squirrel.' Yes, that's correct."

Callings: "Given the questions that you've just answered, is it true the evidence gathered during your investigation established that the President was not involved in the underlying crime related to Russian election interference?"

Muller: "We found insufficient evidence of the President's culpability."

Callings: "So that would be a yes."

Muller: "Pardon?"

Callings: "That would be a yes."

Muller: "I don't guess about anything."

Callings: "I said, THAT WOULD BE A YES!"

Muller: "Uh, what was the question?"

Callings: "I'll move on. Isn't it true the evidence did not establish that the President or those close to him were involved in Russian computer hacking or conspiracies or unlawful relationships with any Russian official, unlike Congressman Swallowell who had an unlawful relationship with a Chinese spy?"

Muller: (sighed) "The answer is in my report."

Callings: "So that's a yes. Is collusion and conspiracy synonymous?"

Muller: "No."

Callings: "In your report, and I quote, "As defined in legal dictionaries, collusion is largely synonymous with conspiracy as that crime is set forth in the general federal conspiracy statute, 18 USC 371."

Muller: "Well, what I'm asking is if you can give me the citation, I can look and evaluate whether it is actually..."

Callings: "OK, let me clarify. I just now stated your report back to you, and when I asked you if collusion and conspiracy were synonymous terms you said no. Are you contradicting your report right now?"

Muller: "Not when I read it."

Callings: "So you want to change your answer to yes then?"

Muller: "No, no... the... if you look at the language..."

Chapter 9

Callings: "I'm reading your report, sir. These are yes or no answers."

Muller: "I... I... I... I leave it with the report."

Callings: "The report says yes, so they are synonymous then."

Muller: "Yes."

Callings: "One last question: Did you ever look into other countries interference into our election? Were other countries investigated who might have interfered in our election?"

Muller: "I'm not going to discuss other matters since I can't remember them anyway."

Callings: "All right. I yield back."

Madler: "Since Mr. Callings has used up the 5 minutes, no more questions will be allowed."

Callings: "But I thought each member of the committee was allowed 5 minutes to ask questions."

Madler: "I specifically stated that only 5 minutes would be allowed for questions, Mr. Callings, and you used up all 5 minutes. I am the chairman and I can make the rules. Adam Shifty taught me that." He then turned to Muller with an arrogant Nancy Lugosi look and said, "Thank you,

147

Director Muller for your scintillating remarks and your inculpatory testimony." He gave the committee a self-assured smile and proudly stated, "30 Days to a More Dynamic Vocabulary." He banged the gavel on his desk and said, "This illustrious committee is now adjourned."

Trumpet Tooted: The phony investigation is over and I was cleared of all charges the Autocrats leveled at me. Now it's my turn.

Chapter 10
The Counter Investigation

BilBar, who looked like the Pilsbury Dough Boy with glasses, had received numerous calls and requests from Rebubbacan congressmen and senators to open a counter investigation into the FBI's *Crossfire Tornado* probe, the FISA documents against Carder Page, the Steel dossier, and Pzok's affair with Leesa Page.

Rebubbacan Representative Devin Noonez had referred eight people to the FBI for investigation regarding "alleged misconduct during the Russia investigation including the leak of classified material and conspiracies to falsify testimony to Congress and the FISA court in order to spy on campaign officials for Trumpet." BilBar wanted to look into that as well. He was brought before the House Appropriate Subcommittee and gave an opening statement:

"As the committee is probably already aware, I am reviewing the FBI's conduct in their investigation of the *Crossfire Tornado* probe, the Carder Page FISA documents, the Steel dossier, and the Pzok/Page affair. I'm trying to get my arms around all the aspects of the counterintelligence investigations that were conducted to see if any illegal spying occurred. As you can see, my arms are pretty short, but I'll do the best I can."

Subcommittee chairman José Surano began the questioning. "Mister Attorney General. Do you honestly think that spying occurred?"

"I think it did," Bilbar replied, "but the question is whether it was appropriately done according to the Geneva Convention. I'm not suggesting that it wasn't, but I want to explore that along with some undersea caves in the Azores on my next cruise."

Surano furrowed his brow like a retiree trying to figure out the answer to a crossword puzzle, then said, "On a different note..." he then pulled out a pitch pipe and blew a C... "it is obvious we could not hold this hearing without mentioning the elephant in the room."

"Are you making a disparaging remark about my weight, Congressman," BilBar asked with a scowl.

"No, I'm referring to the Muller Report," Surano said snidely. "It has come to my attention that some investigators on Muller's team felt that your summary of the Muller Report understated the level of malfeasance by the President and several of his campaign and White House advisers. The American people have been left with many unanswered questions; serious concerns about the

Chapter 10

process by which you formulated your letter commenting about the report and uncertainty about when we can expect to see the full report. I think it would strike a serious blow to our system and yes, even to our very democracy if that unredacted report is not fully produced." He then stood up, waved an American flag while singing one verse of *America The Beautiful*, then sat back down.

BilBar took in a deep breath and said, "Well, the full report can't be exposed to the public due to grand jury information that the intelligence community believes would reveal sources, methods, and information that could interfere with ongoing prosecutions and implicates the privacy or reputational interests of peripheral players where there's a decision not to charge them."

"Would you explain that in simpler terms so even a layman can understand it, Mr. Attorney General?" Surano asked.

"Yes, I'm not releasing the full report, Mr. Layman, I mean, Mr. Chairman."

Autocratic chairwoman Nita Lowy raised her hand and shouted, "Ooo! Ooo!"

Surano raised one eyebrow and said, "The chair recognizes Chairwoman Lowy, who either wants to ask a question or go to the bathroom."

Lowy said, "Thank you, Chairman Surano. First, that was a rousing rendition of *America the Beautiful* you sang and secondly, I do have several questions and comments. Mr. BilBar, your handling of the Muller report has been unacceptable to me and the delay of providing your summary is more suspicious than impressive. "It seems your mind must have already been made up. And what's with all the blacked out areas in the report?"

Bilbar looked at her from under his eyebrows with a

deadpan look and explained, "The blacked out areas are called redactions and they're blacked out to prevent information deemed as privileged or confidential from being read by persons who aren't authorized. I'm sorry you feel that my report has taken longer than you would prefer, but I'm working with Muller and his team through the process and if you know Director Muller, you know he isn't the Flash when it comes to going over testimonies and evidence. What I can do is color code the redacted areas in the report and provide explanatory notes describing the basis for each redaction."

"Oh, that would be marvelous. Could you color code them in pink?" Lowy asked. "Pink is my favorite color."

"I'll see if I have a highliter in pink," BilBar remarked with a mocking smile.

She smirked then asked, "Has Muller or his team reviewed your summary of the report in advance?"

"Muller's team did not play a role in drafting that document but I did give Muller and his team an opportunity to review it. He declined."

"Have you shared any additional information from the report with the White House or has any of Trumpet's administration officials seen the full document?"

"We did advise the White House counsel's office that the letters summarizing the report were being sent and while they weren't given the complete document in advance, it may have been read to them."

"Your summary of the Muller report said that it was inconclusive about whether Trumpet obstructed justice, it also said that it did not exonerate him. Trumpet, meanwhile, has stated publicly that it represented a complete and total exoneration. Which one of you is accurate?"

Chapter 10

"It's hard to have that discussion without the contents of that report, isn't it?" BilBar replied.

Lowy stuck her tongue out at him.

"You know, I'm technically operating under a regulation established under the Clinkton administration, which does not provide for release of the report. I have to rely on my own discretion."

****

Later that night, MSNBC's Rachel Madcow interviewed her special guest.

Madcow: With me tonight is Neal Katyowl, the former acting solicitor general who wrote the regulations regarding the release of redacted reports. Can you explain to our audience what the procedure really is?"

Katyowl: Of course, Rachel. And may I say I watch your show every night and love the way you wrinkle your nose when you disagree with someone."

Madcow: Why, thank you, Neal. May I call you Neal?"

Katyowl: Actually you can call me Squeely Nealy. It's a nickname I received in college. I would go to football games and everytime our team would score, I would squeel. Hence, Squeely Nealy."

Madcow: Yes, thanks for sharing that, Mr. Katyowl. Back to my original question, could you tell us what the procedure is for releasing redacted documents?"

Katyowl: Well, first I have to say I don't agree with Mr. BilBar's explanation. There is no excuse for not releasing the full report. If it reveals sources and methods and information that could interfere with ongoing prosecutions and implicates the privacy or reputational interests of peripheral players where there's a decision not to charge them,...(Whew!) then tough bananas. The public should know what's going on no matter who it hurts."

Madcow looked into the camera and said, "There you have it, folks. BilBar is withholding vital information that the public deserves to know." Turning to her guest, she said, "Thank you, Mr. Katyowl, for being on our show tonight."

Katyowl smiled and said, "That's Squeely Nealy, and also may I add that I've had erotic dreams about you and me..."

The camera flashed back to Madcow who appeared shell-shocked. "We'll be back right after this welcomed commercial break," she quickly said.

****

When BilBar appeared before the Senate Judicious Committee, his opening statement reiterated that he was looking into the FBI probe.

"You know, many people assume the only intelligence collection that occurred was a single confidential informant and a FISA warrant. I'd like to find out whether that's true or not. It strikes me as a fairly weak effort if that was the counterintelligence designed to stop a represented threat."

Rebubbacan Senator John Cornrow asked, "Can you state with confidence that the Steel dossier was not part of the Russian disinformation campaign?"

"No, I'm reviewing that and it's very concerning to me. I don't think it's entirely speculative," BilBar replied, rubbing his chin, with his arm propped up by the other.

"Do you think there were FISA abuses by the Department of Injustice, and FBI?" Cornrow asked.

"These are things I will be looking at and if there was overreach, it occurred with a few people in the higher positions of the FBI and the Department of Injustice, but those people have since conveniently resigned."

Chapter 10

****

Bilbar kicked the counter investigation off by ceremoniously kicking a field goal from the ten yard line at Jack Cook Stadium then appointing a federal prosecutor by the name of John Dourham to assist him. Dourham consequently empaneled his own grand jury and began his investigation by investigating Muller's staff who were investigating Trumpet. He specifically targeted those agents of the FBI who worked on *Crossfire Tornado* before being selected to serve on Muller's team. Streeter Pzok was one of them.

BilBar also asked the Department of Injustice's Inspector General Michael Horrorwitz to examine evidence related to allegations of misconduct regarding FBI Director James Comby's handling of the investigation into Hillery Clinkton's email practices and whether Injustice Department employees leaked information improperly prior to the Presidential election.

Horrorwitz launched the investigation into the FBI and Injustice Department in March. This investigation targeted the FBI and Injustice Department's filing of four FISA applications and renewals to surveil former Trumpet campaign adviser Carder Page and whether or not there was an abuse of this FISA process.

In June, Horrorwitz released his report, concluding that Streter Pzok and other FBI employees brought discredit to themselves and to the agency. He also found that Comby did not follow FBI procedures, but he couldn't determine whether Comby was motivated by political bias or not.

At a July 12 public congressional hearing, Pzok was subpoenaed and asked to explain his personal beliefs expressed in the text messages to Leesa Page. Pzok explained that the text messages he sent to Page were written while he was under the influence of prescription cough syrup and he thought he was sending the texts to his wife. He did say that he was surprised that Americans would vote for a candidate who engaged in such horrible and disgusting behavior, but then half of Americans *were* horrible and disgusting anyway. Pzok swore that the messages in no way meant that he or the FBI, would take any action whatsoever to improperly impact the electoral process for either candidate. Scouts honor. Pzok added that he had information that could have damaged Trumpet before the election but he was such a by-the-book agent that he never ever contemplated leaking it. In his testimony he stated, "To demonstrate my impartiality, I even criticized Clinkton and Slanders during the election. I called Clinkton a vindictive woman and Slanders a crotchety old man. This investigation by the Rebubbacans is misguided and plays into Russia's campaign to tear our country apart." He then stood up and ripped a map of the U.S. in two for effect.

Dourham's investigation produced only two indictments. One for Hillery Clinkton's campaign lawyer and another for the Russian analyst who was a source for the dossier of allegations about Trump. They were indicted separately for allegedly lying to the FBI, and both pleaded not guilty and were given fines of $1 and probation.

Three months later, Horrorwitz released his report stating that he found 17 basic and fundamental errors and omissions in the FBI's applications to the FISA Court, but he did not find political bias during the investigation of Trumpet and Russia, nor did he find evidence that the FBI attempted to place people inside the Trumpet campaign or report on the Trumpet campaign. However, in a

Chapter 10

Senate hearing, Horrorwitz stated he could not rule out political bias as a possible motivation. The report also indicated that the FBI had sufficient factual predication to ask for court approval to begin surveillance of Carder Page. Special agent Pinocchio had been assigned to submit the FISA applications and he testified that everything in the documents was true.

Trumpet Tooted: Horrorwitz's report was far worse than I ever thought possible. He said there was no evidence of political bias by the FBI. Newsflash, Michael! When an agent in the FBI says he's going to make sure I'm not elected, that's textbook political bias. Hello?

Chapter 11
Impeach, Impeach, Impeach

When the Autocratic primaries had concluded, Joe Hiden was their nominee for President. The Autocratic National Committee thought that Hillary was too radioactive to run against Trumpet again and it was rumored they told her to just write a book of excuses why she didn't win.

In the third year of his Presidency, Trumpet made a call to the Ukranian President to congratulate him for winning the Presidential election in Ukrane.

Trumpet: "Congratulations on a great victory, President Zelinski. The way your party came from behind to win was fantastic."

Zelinski: "You are absolutely right Mr. President. Not to brag, but we did win big and destroyed the opposition, mostly with threats. We also wanted to drain the marsh here in our country like you did with yours. We just need bigger pipes."

Trumpet: "Well I think we can send you a few of those. I will say that we do a lot for Ukrane. Much more than the European countries are doing. They should be helping.you more than they are. All Germany does is talk, eat pretzels, and drink beer. The United States, on the other hand, has been very good to Ukrane."

Zelinski: "Yes, you have been. I did talk to the German Chancellor and I did meet with the French President. I told them they are not working as much as they should for Ukrane. The European Union should be our biggest partner but technically the United States is much bigger partner than the European Union. I'm very grateful for your support in the areas of defense, humanitarian

Chapter 11

aid, and animal husbandry."

Trumpet: "Happy to help. I *would* like you to do us a favor if you could, since our country has been through a lot. I heard you had a prosecutor who was very good and he was shut down during an investigation into a company called Burrrizma the Vice President's son was working for. A lot of people here are talking about it. Vice President Hiden bragged he would stop U.S. financial aid to your country unless you stopped the prosecution. A lot of people want to find out why. Whatever you can share with my Attorney General would be great."

Zelinski: "I was going to tell you our new prosecutor will look into the situation, specifically the company that you mentioned. I will personally work on the investigation of the case. If you have any additional information that you can provide to us, it would be very helpful."

Trumpet: "I'll have my people look into it. Good luck with your new administration. Your economy is going to get better and better I predict, especially if you look into that Hiden matter for me."

Zelinski: "I assure you that we will be serious about the case and I will personally work on the investigation. As to the economy, there is much potential for our two countries and one of the issues that is very important for Ukrane is energy independence. I believe we can be very successful cooperating on energy independence with the United States."

Trumpet: "Good. Well, thank you very much and I will tell Rudi and Attorney General Barr to call. Whenever you want to come to the White House, give me a date and we'll work that out."

Zelinski: "Thank you very much, Mr. President. I would be very happy to meet with you personally and look forward to our meeting. I will be in Poland in September. Perhaps we can meet there if you're available."

Trumpet: "I'll see if my schedule will allow it. I like authentic Polish sausage hot dogs."

Zelinski: "Yes, I do as well."

Trumpet: "Before I go, I just want to congratulate you on the fantastic job you're doing and wish you the best."

Zelinski: "Thank you Mr. President. Bye-bye."

When Autocrats learned of the telephone call, they said that Trumpet threatened to hold up aid to Ukrane and other foreign countries unless they provided damaging facts about the Autocratic Party Presidential Primary Candidate, Joe Hiden, as well as information relating to Russian interference in the elections. Trumpet also allegedly enlisted his personal attorney Rudi Jeweliani and Attorney General BilBar, to pressure Ukrane and other foreign governments to cooperate in investigating conspiracy theories begun by the Autocrats concerning Trumpet and his administration.

Trumpet eventually released a payment of a congressionally mandated $400 million military aid package. Zelinski, however, never did release any damaging facts about Hiden in return and had no information about Russian interference in the election.

The phone call was made public in mid-September after an Autocratic whistleblower complained that Trumpet used his Presidential powers to solicit foreign electoral intervention in the U.S. Presidential election. The Autocrats were quick to accuse Trumpet of an illegal and unethical "quid pro quo," unlike Joe Hiden's "quid pro quo" which was certainly ethical and legal.

After it began, a top U.S. diplomat to Ukrane testified he was told that U.S. military aid to Ukrane and

Chapter 11

a Trumpet–Zelinski White House meeting were conditioned on Zelinski publicly announcing investigations into the Hiden family, alleged Ukranian interference in the U.S. elections, and that he liked Polish hot dogs. The European Unions U.S. Ambassador, Gordon Soundland testified that he worked with Jeweliani at Trumpet's "express direction" to put pressure on the Ukrane government. That was enough for Nancy Lugosi to initiate a formal impeachment inquiry into the matter.

In October, three congressional committees deposed witnesses and began an investigation into Trumpet's alleged illegal conduct. The witnesses, all registered Autocrats, testified that President Trumpet wanted Zelinski to publicly announce investigations into Burrrizma, Bunter Hiden, and election interference.

On October 8, the White House officially responded it would not cooperate with the investigation due to concerns that interviews of witnesses were being conducted behind closed doors without Rebubbacans present.

On December 3, the House Unintelligence Committee voted 13 Autocrats to 9 Rebubbacans to adopt a final report and also send it to the House Judicious Committee. The report stated:

"The impeachment inquiry has found that President Trumpet, personally and acting through secret agents within and outside of the U.S. government, solicited the interference of a foreign government, Ukrane, to benefit his re-election. In furtherance of this scheme, President Trumpet coerced the new Ukranian President to begin politically-motivated investigations, including one into President Trumpet's domestic political opponent, Joe Hiden. In pressuring President Zelinski to carry out his demand, President Trumpet withheld a White

House meeting desperately sought by the Ukranian President, and critical U.S. military assistance to fight Russian aggression in Eastern Ukrane. Later he approved the military assistance, but it was only because of the valiant pressure that Autocrats put on him."

The Rebubbacans of the House committees released a contradicting report, saying that the evidence did not support acts of bribery, extortion, or any high crime or misdemeanor by the President. The report also stated that the charges were solely politically motivated and that the Autocrats were trying to impeach a duly elected President based on the accusations and assumptions of unelected bureaucrats who disagreed with President Trumpet's policy initiatives and processes. The President had done nothing wrong and the process was about as fair as a 5', 150 pound white boy playing Lebrawn James one on one.

A set of impeachment hearings was brought before the Judicious Committee, with Trumpet and his lawyers being invited to attend as long as they stood during the entire hearing. Trumpet declined and attended a NATO summit in London instead where he could sit down. On December 6, a letter was sent to Jerry Madler stating the White House would not participate in the impeachment inquiry since it was completely baseless and violated basic principles of due process and origami.

Madler responded, "I gave President Trumpet a fair opportunity to address the overwhelming undisputable evidence before us. After listening to him complain about the impeachment process like a whiny schoolgirl, we had hoped that he might accept our invitation to be grilled like a frozen hamburger. He declined which everyone knows is an indication of guilt and racism."

Chapter 11

The first hearing, held in December, was an academic discussion on the definition of an impeachable offense. The witnesses invited by Autocrats were law professors from Harvard, Stanford, and North Carolina who debated the definition of the word "impeach" for ten hours. Rebubbacans invited a constitutional scholar from George Washington University who testified against impeaching Trumpet, citing a lack of evidence.

Potential articles of impeachment outlined during the hearing included abuse of power for arranging an illegal and unethical quid pro quo with the President of Ukrane, obstruction of Congress for hindering the House's investigation by not coming, and obstruction of justice for attempting to dismiss Robert Muller during his investigation of Russian interference in the election, even though he had only thought about doing it.

On December 5, Nancy Lugosi requested that the House Judicious Committee draft articles of impeachment. After the vote, Lugosi said, "It's a great day for the Constitution, as interpreted by Autocrats, and a sad day for American deplorables who supported Trumpet." She also said, "I could not be prouder or more inspired by the House Autocrats immoral courage, their disreputable methods, and their willingness to misinterpret the requirements of high crimes

and misdemeanors. I always knew how they were going to vote, because I threatened to drain every drop of their blood if they didn't vote the way I wanted them to."

A week later, Autocrats on the House Judiciary Committee announced they would levy two articles of impeachment: (1) abuse of power, and (2) obstruction of Congress in its investigation of the President's conduct regarding Ukrane.

On December 13, the Judicious Committee voted to pass both articles of impeachment with all Autocrats present voting in support and all Rebubbacans opposing.

On December 16, the House Judicious Committee released a 658-page report on the articles of impeachment, specifying criminal bribery and wire fraud charges as part of the abuse of power article. The articles were forwarded to the full House for debate and a vote on whether to impeach the President.

The formal impeachment vote in the House of Representatives took place on December 18. Shortly after 8:30 pm EST, both articles of impeachment passed. The votes for the charge of abuse of power were 230 in favor, 197 against, and 1 present. All House Rebubbacans voted against. The votes for the charge of obstruction of Congress were 229 in favor, 198 against, and 1 present. All Rebubbacans voted against.

That night Trumpet Tooted: "Why should Vampira Lugosi be allowed to Impeach the President of the United States, just because she has a slight majority in the House and her fangs are longer than anyone elses? There was no crime. The call I made to the President of Ukrane was perfect, and there was no pressure on my part. This Scam Impeachment is very unfair with no due process, proper

Chapter 11

representation, or witnesses for my defense. Now Lugosi is demanding the Senate investigation be run by Autocrat rules. What a bunch of marsh scum!"

****

In mid-December, with the support of all 47 Senate Autocrats, Minority Leader Chuck Shoemer wrote a letter to Rebubbacan Majority Leader, Mitch McColonel calling for several men in Trumpet's administration to testify in a pre-trial proceeding to take place on January 6. Two days later, McColonel rejected the call for witnesses to testify, saying that the Senate's role is simply to act as "judge and jury" and not to help the Autocrats. He also suggested that witnesses be called during the trial, as had happened after Bill Clinkton's impeachment. Shoemer said that he did not hear a single word, sentence, paragraph, or outline as to why the witnesses should not give testimony.

McColonel replied, "Who do you think you are? My speech coach?"

On the day of the impeachment, Lugosi declined to comment on when the impeachment resolution would be given to the Senate and said, "So far we haven't seen anything that looks beneficial to us." The following day, McColonel met with Shoemer briefly to discuss the trial and play rock, paper, scissors for who would make the Senate rules. McColonel won. After the Senate reconvened from its one month holiday break, Lindsey Grahamcracker proposed that he and McColonel change the rules of the Senate so they could start the trial without Lugosi, since it would be at night and that's when Lugosi looked for her victims.

McColonel announced the senate had passed a blueprint for the trial, which discussed witnesses and evidence after the opening arguments. Lugosi called for the resolution to be published before she could proceed with the next steps, but McColonel told her to pound sand.

In mid-January, the House approved the articles of impeachment to be sent to the Senate. Lugosi then led a procession of the managers and other House officers across the Capitol building accompanied by a funeral dirge played on a boom box carried by Adam Shifty, to where the impeachment was announced to the senate. The House's involvement in the impeachment process came to an end, thank goodness.

Before the trial, McColonel told Sean Handitee of Foxy News that there was no chance Trumpet would be convicted, expressing his hope that all Senate Rebubbacans would acquit the President of both charges.

The House managers, acting as prosecutors for the case, were several Autocratic representatives, the most infamous were Adam Shifty and Jerry Madler. Trumpet named his defense team of several prominent Rebubbacans, then the trial rules were voted on. At the end of the session, McColonel's proposed trial rules were passed by the Rebubbacan majority and the Autocratic amendments rejected.

On the first day, the prosecution's opening arguments and presentation of evidence took place. Their argument was that Trumpet demanded a quid pro quo from the Ukranian President or he would withold aid. Trumpet's defense presentation based its argument on the premise that there was no direct evidence of wrongdoing, aid was released without Ukrane responding to Trumpet's request, and that Autocrats were attempting to use the impeachment to steal the upcoming election.

When the prosecutors and defense team had concluded their arguments, the Senate voted and acquitted

Chapter 11

Trumpet on both counts of misconduct. Mitt Rotney was the first senator in history from an impeached President's party to vote "guilty" on the first count.

Before the trial, Americans were sharply divided on whether Trumpet should be removed from office, with Autocrats largely supporting removal and Rebubbacans largely opposing. Independents were divided.

A poll released on the day of Trumpet's impeachment found that the President's approval rating increased by six points during the process, while support for the impeachment fell.

Two days after he was acquitted by the Senate in the impeachment trial, Trumpet fired two witnesses who testified in the impeachment inquiry about his conduct.

The impeachment of Donald Trumpet was over. Autocrats still had other existential threats to eliminate in their own minds. However, now the country had to face a real existential threat.

That night Trumpet Tooted: "The sham impeachment is finally over The Autocrats had absolutely no evidence and it was strictly a political move by them to punish me for not giving in to all of their socialist demands. It's disgraceful and they should have been directing their attention to passing helpful legislation for the American people instead of wasting time on the phony impeachment."

Chapter 12
Does Anyone Know Where the China Virus Came From?

While Trumpet was being impeached and Autocrats swore he was a threat to American democracy, a real threat was quietly making its way into our country. An outbreak of a deadly virus spread across the Chinese city of Woohan. Alleged attempts by the Chinese government to contain it failed, allowing the virus to spread to the U.S. and all across the globe.

The initial reports stated that it began in a wet market in Woohan from diseased animals that people ate. Pangolins and bats were the two animals that the Chinese government-run media named. The U.S. mainstream media later reported that it could have come from chipmunks and cats. No one in the mainstream media or Autocratic Party believed it could have originated in the Woohan Institute of Virology that studied the exact virus that just happened to be unleashed on the world. No, that was too coincidental.

The World Health Overlords (WHO) declared a

Chapter 12

Public Health Emergency of International Concern on January 30, and called the virus COBID-19, also dubbing it as the "Bolona Virus."

The symptoms most commonly included fever, dry cough, fatigue, and a strong urge to visit Bolona, Italy. Severe illness were more likely in elderly patients and those with certain underlying medical conditions. The virus was transmitted from person to person by small airborne particles containing the virus. The risk was highest when people were in close proximity or closed in spaces. Transmission occurred when contaminated fluids reached the eyes, nose or mouth. Infected persons were typically contagious for 10 days, and could spread the virus even if they didn't develop symptoms.

At first, the virus was dismissed by Autocrats as nothing more than a bad cold. Nancy Lugosi even encouraged people to go out and have fun in San Francisco's China Town, especially at night so she could have more "blood donors" to choose from.

When the first case was discovered in the U.S., Trumpet established a task force specifically to disseminate information about the virus and inform the public about what the White House was doing to try and prevent it from spreading. He asked the Director of the National Institute of All Infectious Diseases to head the task force and called a press conference near the end of January.

Trumpet: I'd like to thank the press for attending this important briefing. I've created a task force to make recommendations as to the course of action our country should pursue regarding this virus. First, I want to introduce the leading member of the team I have put together, Tony Fowchi. Tony, would you like to say a few words to our phony press?"

Fowchi: "Of course, I never pass up an opportunity to step into the spotlight, and that's *Doctor* Tony Fowchi if you don't mind." He gave Trumpet a derisive look then cleared his throat. "For those of you who don't know me, I am the world's most renown physician/scientist and immunologist currently serving as the director of the National Institute of All Infectious Diseases and the Chief Medical Advisor to the President. There is nothing about allergies and infectious diseases that I don't know... or do know... I always get those two comparisons confused. Anyway, I have been assigned by the President to make a statement about this virus. Right now it's not a major threat and the risk to the American public is low. But we'll keep our eye on it. Nothing to worry about, the symptoms are like catching a bad cold and wanting to visit Italy."

Reporter: "So you don't think the public should worry about it?"

Fowchi: "Naw, just wash your hands and gargle regularly. The President has instituted some travel restrictions to China which I think is a good idea. We're not sure just how dangerous this virus is yet and China won't allow anyone into their country anyway. They're just letting people out. Back to you, Mr. President."

****

At a Trumpet rally in February, the President said, "If this virus is like a cold, which Fowchi thinks it is, it will be gone by April when the weather gets warmer."

The next day, Fowchi was on CBS and said, "I don't remember saying the virus is like a cold, but it is a stretch for the President to assume it will disappear in the summer. Right now the risk is still low for people to get seriously ill, so just keep washing and gargling."

Chapter 12

At a briefing in March, Trumpet announced: "I've just been told that a drug called hydroxychlorophyll has been producing some great results against the virus and could be a game changer to relieve the symptoms. What do you think, Tony?"

Fowchi raised his eyebrows and looked up. "Purely anecdotal evidence that a lay person like you would accept as fact. On the other hand, I have noticed people around town wearing surgical masks. I would discourage doing that, since the evidence doesn't support it being helpful and you might get shot by the police who could assume you just robbed a liquor store. Besides, if everybody wore a surgical mask, the hospitals could run out and they'd have to use Halloween masks which could traumatize the patients."

To Fowchi's dismay, the number of people infected by the virus quickly grew, which caused Trumpet to declare a national emergency. Governments around the world required mask mandates for everyone and ordered law enforcement agencies to enforce them. Panic buying caused widespread supply shortages. Global lockdowns were instituted to slow the spread and educational institutions and public areas were partially or fully closed in many jurisdictions. Trumpet rallies were cancelled or postponed, but BLM and ANTIFA demonstrations were allowed because they were protesting for democracy and everyone knows viruses won't attack people protesting for demoracy. Conflicting stories circulated through social media and mainstream media, and political tensions intensified. Rebubbacans blamed Autocrats for providing misinformation to the media and Autocrats blamed Rebubbacans for providing sensible information to the public.

Foxy News' dogmatic commentator Sean Handitee reported one night:

"Well, as usual, the Autocrats managed to get their priorities backwards. Instead of taking seriously a deadly pandemic, they thought the sham impeachment of a Rebubbacan President was more important. Nancy, I hope you're happy that you've allowed the deaths of thousands of our people just so you could say you impeached Donald Trumpet. Was the kudo worth it?"

On CNN, Kwis Chromo reported:

"You know who is responsible for spreading this virus. It's the Trumpet supporters. Every time they have a rally, they sneeze and cough on each other, hoping to spread it to liberals. They don't mind if a few of them die as long as they can get rid of anyone who opposes their misguided ideology. My brother, the governor of New York, is one of many liberal governors trying to keep people safe. He has instituted a program to put those who have contracted COBID into rest homes so they can't spread it to people on the street. Sheer genius, even if he does have nasal passages the size of volleyballs."

At the next COBID briefing, Fowchi announced some new rules:

"Since we now know that COBID-19 is an airborne transmitted virus, I am advising everyone from here on out to stay in your homes, except for those who work in essential businesses such as online stores like Amazone and all liquor stores. Those businesses can remain open; all other businesses should shut their doors. People can work from their homes, have their groceries delivered by drones, and their kids can school at home on computers taught by teachers on Zume, once they return from their extended vacations. Don't, I repeat, *don't* go outside or to the gym. If you want to exercise or walk your dog, every home should order a treadmill. Any questions?"

Chapter 12

Reporter: "Yes. What about people who don't have computers or treadmills and can't afford them?"

Fowchi: "Schools will provide them as part of the inflated student loan program. Next question."

Reporter: "Why did you agree to head the President's task force when he's such a racist?"

Fowchi: "Because I get paid lots of money. Next question."

Reporter: "How much are you paid?"

Fowchi: "Next question."

Reporter: "What specific measures is the government taking to eliminate this virus before it kills us all?"

Fowchi: "Good question. Next question."

The reporters all looked at each other and shrugged their shoulders. When no one else spoke up, Fowchi smiled like he had just looted a Walgreen's store and said, "Back to you, Mr. President."

Trumpet: "Thank you, Tony, for that, uh, informative briefing. Now, as all of you know, this China virus is nasty so we are going to have to take some precautions like Tony said if we want to keep it from spreading."

Reporter: "Why are you calling it the China virus. Don't you know that's racist and makes you sound like a xenophobe?"

Trumpet: "I call it the China virus because it comes from *China*."

Reporter: "How do you know it came from China? Some of our best scientific minds say it could have originated from Americans who were bitten by Chinese bats."

Trumpet: "Where do Chinese bats come from?"

Reporter: "Oh."

Shortly afterwards Fowchi appeared on MSNBC's *The Rachel Madcow Show*:

Madcow: "Tonight we have Anthony Fowchi on the show who has some new information about the virus. Dr. Fowchi, what can you tell us?"

Fowchi: "Well, Rachel, it appears that the virus is more deadly than I first estimated so I'm proposing some new guidelines. If people absolutely have to go outside for necessities, they need to wear three masks and keep apart from each other a distance of at least ten feet. We can have Bolona Virus referees that will flag violators for being offside and they will have to spend ten days in a cardboard penalty box."

Madcow: "That sounds like a brilliant plan, Doctor. I noticed you called COBID-19 the Bolona Virus. Does that mean the virus originated in Italy and not China?"

Fowchi: "Oh, no. Ha, ha... that's a good one, Rachel."

Madcow: "You never know, Trumpet's deplorables might believe that it does and boycott pizza, spaghetti, and Italian bread."

Fowchi: "That's the least of my worries right now, Rachel. I have a lot more appearances to make in order to reach my goal of exorbitant guest fees for this year."

Madcow: "Well, good luck on your 'guest quest,' Doctor, and you're always welcome to come back anytime."

Fowchi: "Thank you, Rachel, you've been a gracious host, or should I say hostess? What should I call you?"

Madcow: "Gay woman will do."

****

When Trumpet found out about Fowchi's appearance on the Madcow show, he said: "Fowchi's proposal isn't realistic because we don't have enough qualified COBID referees, masks, or cardboard boxes. We have to order all that from China."

Chapter 12

Although Fowchi was praised by those on the left, he was criticized by the right.

Dan Bongoni of Foxy News said: "So if you take your wife out for dancing, how are you going to dance slow with her if you have to stay ten feet away from each other? And if you're wearing 3 masks, how are you going to kiss her? You didn't think that one over too carefully, did you, Lord of the Masks?"

Laura Ingrum of Foxy News said: "Now Fowchi wants us to wear three masks and stay ten feet apart from one another? At first, masks weren't necessary now they're essential. In a few weeks, Fowchi will require that surfers wear masks while they're surfing or they'll be arrested. The mask requirement is nothing but a liberal plot to keep American citizens terrified, and that's the angle."

On CNN Jim Acostya interviewed Fowchi.

Acostya: "Dr. Fowchi, the death toll in the United States seems to be climbing, especially in New York rest homes. It appears that Trumpet's policies aren't working."

Fowchi: "Right at the beginning I wanted to shut everything down, but the President gave me a lot of pushback against it. He said it was imperative that schools and non-essential businesses stay open. I told him kids could put off their education for awhile and if a few restaurants had to close their doors permanently, that was better than having people die of a COBID-grilled steak."

Acostya: "Dr. Fowchi I couldn't have said it better. Speaking of steaks, after the show, you're invited over to my house for a nice Kobe filet. It'll only cost you $400."

Fowchi: "Jim, you're too kind. I'll bring the wine, a Napa Valley Cabernet Sauvignon. It'll only cost you $5,000."

Acostya: "Oh, I just remembered, I have a dental

appointment tonight. We'll have to do it another time."

Fowchi: "After the pandemic is over, maybe we can roast a couple of hot dogs and some marshmallows."

Acostya: "Yeah, it's probably better if we do that."

****

For the next few months, Fowchi and Trumpet seemed to contradict each other and virus infections soared to an all-time high.

To celebrate the Fourth of July, Trumpet arranged for a fireworks display at Mount Rushmore. The public was invited. Fowchi warned, "Everyone who goes is going to die."

After the celebration, when no one died, Trumpet publicly announced that Fowchi made a lot of mistakes and called him Phony Tony.

In a hearing before a senate committee, Senator Rand Pall asked Fowchi, "Do you have any second thoughts about your mitigation recommendations for the U.S.? In comparison, Sweden has had more success without implementing the severe restrictions you have proposed."

Fowchi stood by his guidelines. "For your information, Senator, and I use the

Chapter 12

term 'Senator' loosely, Sweden's fatality rate has exceeded those of other Scandinavian countries. So there."

Pall replied, "What's that got to do with your recommendations for *our* country?"

"My recommendations remain valid for our country, not Sweden," Fowchi stated jutting his chin out. "And besides, my approval rating is higher than the President's."

"What about New York's high fatality rate? Wouldn't that indicate your methods were insufficient, Doctor, and I use the term 'Doctor' loosely?"

"You've misconstrued that, Senator, New York is just one state."

"Then how about California, Florida, Texas, Michigan, Ohio..."

"You're cherry picking, Senator," Fowchi responded.

"I don't even like cherries!" Pall stated vehemently.

"Are you finished with your baseless accusations?" Fowchi grumbled as he checked his guest appearance schedule on his phone.

Pall regained his composure and said, "I have one last question. Some respected virologists have stated they believe the virus came from the Woohan Institute of Virology lab where Chinese virologists were conducting gain of function research on bat Bolona viruses. Didn't your organization fund them to study those viruses?"

Fowchi turned red in the face and pointed a hypodermic needle at Pall. "My organization has never funded gain-of-function research in the Woohan Institute of Virology or any other institute of virology."

Pall smiled self-assuredly at Fowchi and said, "I have a statement from a well-qualified coworker in your organization that says you *do* fund gain of function research at the Woohan lab."

Fowchi's face twisted like a pretzel. Jumping to his feet, he shouted, "That's a clinical lie! My organization doesn't have any well-qualified people working in it."

Pall sat back in his chair and shook his head. Needless to say, not much was accomplished.

****

Then came the day when Trumpet contracted CO-BID-19. He went on the air and announced that he and Melonia had tested positive for the virus. They both were taken to Ralter Weed Hospital to undergo treatment. The reaction from the Trumpet-haters on the mainstream media was immediate.

Whoopie Coldburger on *The Slanted View* talk show, said, "I don't believe that he actually contracted the virus. I think he's just saying that to get sympathy since his approval rating is in the toilet."

Joi Bayhar agreed and said, "He's related to Pootin and his wife is half Russian. How can you believe anything he says?"

Tooter had to delete a number of Toots wishing the President would succumb to the virus, but gave raises to the employees who initially posted them.

Three days later Trumpet was back in the White House, much to the dismay of the progressive social and mainstream media and the vile Tooting anti-Trumpeters.

***The night the President returned from the hospital, he Tooted:** "Thanks to the great doctors and therapeutics they gave Melonia and me, I feel great and look forward to getting on the campaign trail. If the left wing whackos can have their demonstrations, I can have my rallies."*

Chapter 13
The Summer of Our Discontent

MINNESOTA

On May 25, Trumpet's final year in office, Foxy News reported: A white Minneapolis police officer arrested a black man for trying to pass a counterfeit twenty dollar bill. The man resisted at one point and the officer restrained him by holding his knee on the man's neck for several minutes. Despite the man's shouts that he couldn't breathe, the officer kept his knee on his neck. The man died as a result. However, the autopsy showed the main cause of death was a large quantity of fentanyl in his system. The video of the officer kneeling on his neck went viral and people took to the streets to protest police brutality.

Organizations such as ANTIFA, Black Lives Madder, and other activists who sympathized with those groups, set fires and ransacked stores in protest. An

MSNBC reporter even stated that protests were mostly peaceful as a huge building fire raged in the background.

At one point, rioters cheered as people also set a Minneapolis police precinct headquarters on fire after the department was forced to abandon it.

MSNBC Joyless Reed reported on the incident with the police officer and the black man as follows:

"MSNBC viewers it's a sad day in our country. A racist white police officer intentionally killed an unarmed black man by kneeling on his neck to demonstrate white superiority over the black race. It exemplifies the systemic racism that has swept over our country and is threatening to take us back to the days of segregation, discrimination and Jim Crow. Fortunately, peaceful demonstrators protested this heinous act of systemic racism by sitting around numerous campfires in Minneapolis singing songs of black solidarity and helping stores and shops in the area get rid of hard-to-sell merchandise by volunteering to take the items off their hands. What thoughtfulness.

Protesters even visited a Minneapolis police headquarters to have a constructive discussion with the police. Unfortunately, the meeting resulted in fiery dialogue between the two groups and the police left the meeting abruptly, unwilling to discuss ways to improve the relationship between law enforcement and the black community. Yesterday, white supremacy reared its ugly head again and unless our black brothers and sisters do something about these unwarranted attacks by police on innocent black people, more blacks will become victims of police brutality and the black race will become extinct. Black activists everywhere, start putting our knees on the necks of white racists and make *them* scream for air.

Chapter 13
NEW YORK

Foxy News reported: Violence and lawlessness continued in other parts of the country. Mobs rampaged down the sidewalks of New York, smashing into numerous luxury shops to steal merchandise. Hundreds of people marauded through the area, breaking into boutiques as well as clothing and electronics stores taking what they wanted. The smash-and-grab sprees and sporadic unrest forced New York City officials to impose a citywide curfew for several days, which led to clashes between protesters and police officers attempting to clear the streets.

On CNN, Brian "Alka" Seltzer, reported:

"In response to the black man that was executed in Minneapolis by a white racist police officer, people in New York also took to the streets to peacefully protest that act of systemic racism. To show their support, shops allowed protesters to take whatever items they wanted and were delighted when demonstrators helped remodel their stores. One shop owner stated: 'I've been wanting to take out that ugly front window for a long time so I'm glad a few young men helped me get rid of it. Now I can put up plywood across the front of the store which will make my establishment much more secure.'

The New York Black Lives Madder group also participated in the demonstration and showed their opposition to high incidents of police brutality by marching down the streets chanting, 'Pigs in a frying pan, fryem' like sausage.' I wish I hadn't finished with that, now I'm hungry." Looking off camera, Seltzer said, "Somebody get me a donut. Make that a dozen."

OREGON

Foxy News reported: "Portland, Oregon's largest

city, saw more than one hundred consecutive nights of racial injustice protests marred by vandalism, chaos and violence.

The demonstrations that started in late May divided residents and flared even further in July when President Trumpet deployed federal law enforcement agents to stop attacks on a federal courthouse and other U.S. property.

Thousands of demonstrators turned out nightly, with some hurling fireworks, rocks, ball bearings and bottles at the agents. They responded with huge plumes of tear gas, rubber bullets and flash-bang grenades that created chaotic, war zone-like scenes.

Those clashes with federal agents ended July 31, when state police took over from U.S. agents under a deal brokered by the governor and the U.S. Department of Homeland Security. But smaller protests continued, with groups of 100 to 200 people marching nightly.

Protesters called for city officials to slash the police budget and reallocate that money to Black residents and businesses. Some also called for the resignation of the Mayor.

During the clashes, some broke windows, set small fires, punctured police car tires with spikes, shined lasers in officers' eyes and pelted them with rocks and frozen water bottles.

In August, protesters were seen on video punching and kicking a white man to the ground after he crashed his truck onto the sidewalk.

Video posted online of the incident showed the man sitting in the street next to the truck. A crowd gathered around him and repeatedly punched and kicked him in the head.

Witnesses told police the man had been helping a

transgender woman who had an item of hers stolen before he got into his truck and drove off. He sped away as protesters, some of whom were in the street, could be seen on video kicking his car. After crashing, he was dragged out of the car and beaten by nine or ten people. When police arrived the man was bloodied and unconscious. He later recovered from his injuries.

Tensions reached a new high at the end of that month, when a pro-Trumpet caravan motored into downtown, with some occupants shooting paintballs and spraying bear repellent at Black Lives Madder protesters who tried to block the streets.

Fistfights broke out and, as night fell, a Trumpet supporter was fatally shot as he walked on a sidewalk. The suspected shooter was later killed by a law enforcement task force sent to arrest him outside Lacey, Washington."

An ABC news correspondent reported:

"Portland, known for its peaceful liberal approaches to just about everything, joined in with demonstrators across the nation to celebrate a racial awakening by shooting off fireworks, some which accidentally struck the police gestapo crowd control units. Upset by the accidental discharges, police responded by firing tear gas, rubber bullets and flash bang grenades injuring several protesters.

Peaceful protests continued, as demonstrators shared ice cold water bottles with police since it was hot, and put spikes on their police car tires so they could be prepared for winter weather. BLM and ANTIFA provided entertainment, including boxing and karate exhibitions, and a laser show especially for police. A few protesters were injured, however, when they were assaulted by anti-protesters and one pro-Trumpet man was killed, who was mistaken for a bear. Protesters also started a campfire in the downtown area to roast marshmallows. When one passer-by commented that it was a pretty big fire to roast marshmallows, a protester stated, 'They're big marshmallows.'

CHICAGO

Foxy News reported: "With tensions already heightened following police shootings of black subjects, hundreds, if not thousands of people descended on downtown Chicago in August following another police shooting on the city's South Side.

Vandals smashed the windows of a dozen businesses and made off with merchandise, cash machines and virtually anything else they could carry.

The police superintendent told reporters that the shooting of the man who had opened fire on officers apparently prompted a social media post that urged people to form a car caravan and converge on the business and shopping district.

"Car caravans" of looters made their way into Chicago's upscale neighborhoods and neighboring commercial districts.

Over several hours, police made more than 100 arrests and 13 officers were injured, including one who was struck in the head with a bottle.

Occupants in a vehicle opened fire on police who were arresting a man they spotted carrying a cash register.

Vehicles drove away slowly, some leaving behind boxes of rocks that they had apparently brought to shatter the windows. Cash register drawers and clothes hangers were strewn about the streets, along with ATMs that had been ripped from walls or pulled from inside businesses.

Stores miles from downtown were also ransacked, their parking lots littered with glass and boxes that once contained television sets and other electronics.

Weeks earlier in July, a downtown protest over a statue devolved into a chaotic scene of police swinging batons and demonstrators hurling frozen water bottles, fireworks and other projectiles at officers.

An NBC reporter gave the following account:

"The reaction to police shootings of blacks was evident in the city today. Hundreds of protesters took to the downtown streets after a black man was shot by police on the south side. Although the man shot at police first, witnesses say the police should have cited him for unlawful discharge of a firearm. Demonstrators patronized dozens of shops seeking donations to help the impoverished families of the slain black man and received clothing, electronics, and cash machines to help poor victims of systemic racism. Earlier in July, protesters gathered at a statue of Christopher Columbus to assist city officials in moving it to a better site like the Chicago River. Police came to supervise and were thrown ice cold bottles of water by the demonstrators to cool off and treated to a horizontal fireworks display. Demonstrators also passed out bricks and one officer was heard to say, 'Gee, this is great. I wanted to build a brick fire pit at my house and the demonstrators donated enough for me to finish it off. I plan on getting started as soon as I get out of the hospital.'"

WISCONSIN

Foxy News reported: "Protests erupted in August following the police shooting of a black man shot multiple times while three of his children looked on.

His shooting was caught on video by a man who reportedly said he saw the man scuffling with three officers who had been called on a domestic disturbance and heard them yell, "Drop the knife! Drop the knife!" before the gunfire erupted.

In the footage, the black man walked from the sidewalk around the front of his SUV to his driver-side door as officers followed him with their guns drawn shouting at him. As the man opened the door and leaned into the SUV to grab a knife, an officer grabbed his shirt from behind and opened fire. Seven shots could be heard in the footage.

The man's family later revealed he was paralyzed as a result of the shooting.

The shooting sparked protests over racial injustice in several cities, which devolved into unrest and riots.

Crowds destroyed dozens of buildings and set more than 30 fires in downtown Kenoshuh. In one instance, a Kenoshuh car dealership reportedly sustained $1.5 million in damage during one night of riots.

Tensions flared further when a 17-year-old killed two protesters who attacked him.

The teenager was charged with first-degree intentional homicide in the killing of the two protesters and attempted intentional homicide in the wounding of a third. He also faced a misdemeanor charge of underage firearm possession for wielding a semiautomatic rifle.

The incident occurred on the night of Aug. 25, when he was in Kenoshuh with a friend. The young man said he was there that night to protect a business and also "to help people."

According to prosecutors and court documents, he shot and killed a 36-year-old Kenoshuh man, after the man threw a plastic bag containing unknown items at the teenager, then tried to wrestle his rifle away.

While trying to get away in the immediate aftermath, the teenager was captured on cellphone video saying, "I just killed somebody." According to the complaint filed by prosecutors, someone in the crowd said, "Beat him up!" and another yelled, "Get him! Get that dude!"

Video shows that the teenager tripped in the street. As he was on the ground, a 26-year-old hit him with a skateboard and tried to take his rifle. The teenager opened fire, killing the man and wounding another who pointed a handgun at him.

Cellphone video that captured some of the action shows that right after the shootings, the teenager walked slowly toward a police vehicle with his hands up, only to be waved through by police.

He returned to his Illinois home and turned himself in soon after. Police later blamed the chaotic conditions for why they didn't arrest him at the scene.

His attorneys and family insisted he was only defending himself when he fired the gun, which belonged to a friend.

CNN's Vaina Bash commented on the incident concerning the black man shot by the police in the domestic disturbance and the Kenoshuh shootings as follows:

"A black man was shot and killed by police as he attempted to get into his car. When the police chief was asked why his officers shot the man, he stated that the man grabbed a knife from his car and the officers felt threatened. A witness stated that the knife wasn't even sharp from what he could see 30 feet away and it didn't even look real. 'It looked more like a banana,' the man was quoted to say. Just another example of police overreacting and using deadly force when they could have easily subdued the man.

In Kenoshuh, Wisconsin demonstrators marched in protest to systemic racism and were confronted by a young man carrying a semi-automatic rifle, another illegal weapon of war. The young man, a white supremacist thirsting for blood, killed two men who might have been black, and wounded a third who tried to stop him from killing more people. It's a miracle only two brave demonstrators were killed."

Later, Vaina Bash reported: "The young man who shot two people and wounded another in the Kenoshuh, Wisconsin peaceful demonstration went to trial today. He is charged with first degree murder, among other charges, and should receive capital punishment for his senseless and heinous crimes. I don't usually believe in capital punishment, but in this case, I'll make an exception. There was a tense moment in the courtroom when one of the defense attorneys pointed the rifle at a juror and said, 'Bang! You're dead! How would you like to be the recipient of that?' The juror fainted and had to be revived with smelling salts."

Even later, Don Leman of CNN reported: "The trial of the 17 year old who shot and killed two people and wounded one in Kenoshuh, Wisconsin during a peaceful demonstration, was surprisingly acquitted today. His defense attorneys based their case on self-defense while the prosecuting attorneys based their case on the fact he didn't live in Kenoshuh, had no business helping people there, he didn't own the rifle, and he almost shot some black people. Just the fact that the defendant was seen with a white supremacist group in a photo should have been enough to put him in prison for the rest of his life."

Chapter 13
PENNSYLVANIA

Foxy News reported: "Demonstrators took to the streets of Philadelphia following the October officer-involved shooting of an armed black man with a knife reportedly with a mental health history.

The man's family said he was experiencing a mental health crisis when police were called.

Officers who arrived at the scene fired 14 shots after the man advanced toward the officers despite their orders that he drop the knife. The shooting was caught on video.

More than a thousand people took to the streets following the shooting, ransacking big-name stores as well as smaller businesses. Hundreds were arrested, and dozens of police and law enforcement vehicles were damaged during the riots.

Meanwhile, more than 50 police officers were injured, including a sergeant who was intentionally run over by a pick-up truck driver.

MSNBC reported: "Police shoot a mentally ill black man. The man's family said he was playing mumblety peg and the police thought he was going to throw the knife at them. Demonstrators took to the streets of Philadelphia and went on shopping sprees to alleviate the depression they felt. Unfortunately, one of the shoppers forgot his money and tried to flee the scene with his goods. Police responded and 50 officers were injured trying to stop him, one who had his foot run over."

****

Black Lives Madder advocated that there were more effective methods of providing safety to our communities—methods that opposed the murder and brutalization of black people by police. One of these methods was decriminalization. BLM wanted to repeal outdated laws that did not serve the black community like robbery, burglary, drunk driving, and assault. By prioritizing public health and social support, reliance on enforcement could be eliminated they proposed. They also proposed that police should be disarmed, demilitarized, and have less technology available to them. They insisted that SWAT teams increased fear, not safety, and by taking away military-grade weapons and invasive technologies from police, cities could develop more non-violent solutions to social problems like darts with sedatives and bribes given to lawbreakers as an incentive to be good.

To embrace this new ideology, many cities began to cut police budgets, resulting in fewer officers on the beats. Then to be less punitive to the poor criminal who society had forced into a life of crime, progressive well-funded entities began supporting the election of lenient district attorneys who changed the way they prosecuted criminal offenses. Some felonies were reduced to misdemeanors and bail was done away with in many cases. Criminals were given a second chance, a third chance, and as many chances as they wanted to start over. Victims, on the other hand, got only one chance... if they lived.

Looting became acceptable for those who considered themselves oppressed by systemic white racism.

Those who committed arson and property destruction during "mostly peaceful demonstrations" were released on bail and their fines paid by progressive billionaires and Autocratic politicians.

Trumpet Tooted: It's funny how liberal anarchists practically destroy many of our cities through rioting and the liberal politicians and media don't say a word about it. They're too busy impeaching Presidents and putting out phony news I guess.

Chapter 14
Where's Joe?

As summer turned into fall and swim suits turned into sweat suits, Trumpet hit the road, speaking to massive crowds in large venues all across the country. Joe's handlers, on the other hand, played a masterful game of hide and seek. If Joe couldn't be heard, he couldn't commit any verbal faux pas. When he did hit the road for the few appearances he had, he spoke to all the socially distanced masked crowds that could fit in a mini-mart parking lot.

In October, Trumpet held a massive rally in Allentown, Pennsylvania attended by several thousand people.

Trumpet approached the podium amidst cheers and shouts of "Where's Joe?" and "Four more years!"

Trumpet put up his hands to quiet the crowd then said, "Thank you very much, Allentown. I want to begin today by discussing an issue of existential importance to Pennsylvania. No, it's not climate change. Last week, Tired Joe made perhaps the most shocking admission ever uttered in the history of Presidential debates. Besides admitting he eats spaghetti noodles through his nose, Joe confirmed his plan to abolish the entire US oil industry. That means no fracking, no jobs, no energy for Pennsylvania families, Texas, and all the others who depend on oil for their livelihood. He said he wanted to break wind, or maybe he meant go with wind energy. I can just see brownouts and blackouts all over Pennsylvania now. I guess if you had a blackout, you couldn't see. Anyway, he wants to replace oil rigs with windmills that are made in Germany and China. They send carbon into the air when they're making them and dead birds in the air after they're made when they're hit by the blades.

Tired Joe's plan is an economic death sentence for Pennsylvania's energy sector. He will send Pennsylvania into a crippling depression and prices on everything will skyrocket. An energy shutdown would cause massive layoffs, soaring gas prices, surging energy bills, no air conditioning in the summer, no heat during the winter, no electricity during peak hours, and record obesity in dogs and cats.

Did you see Joe's running mate, Camela Heiress last night on television? What's with the hysterical laugh? She was asked a horrible question about herself and she just cackled like a hyena. And when it comes to being liberal, she's more liberal than Bonkers Berney. She even sponsored the $100 trillion Green New Steal plan that Congresswomen Ocasional Cortez, Ilhand Omy, Aywanna Pressyou, and Rashonme Tobleed known as *The Squat* advocated. Joe wants to ship your energy jobs to foreign polluters all over China and the rest of the world. It was

Chapter 14

hard enough bringing them back, but I managed to do it. Actually, a lot of our jobs are coming back now. As you know, many people that were shut out of their jobs resorted to suicide, drugs, alcohol, and watching re-runs of *The Andy Griffin Show*.

Have you seen the opinion polls? It's funny, but whenever I have good opinion polls, the phony news stations won't accept them. They won't put them out unless they're negative. Remember four years ago, I used to read the opinion polls. I'd drive the Autocrats crazy and they'd say, "Oh, that's not right," but it turned out to be right. The Autocrat officials in Allentown even tried to prevent me from holding a rally here, saying they didn't have a venue I could use. But we didn't give up and just got this thing literally hours ago. And to have people across the street trying to get in is amazing. I mean, it's more amazing than people being let out of jail by progressive D.A.'s. Well, maybe not that amazing.

I watched CNN this morning and heard, "COBID, COBID, COBID. Don't go and vote or you'll die. Mail your ballots. In fact, mail a bunch of them." If you look at some of these early opinion polls, we're supposed to be way down because of fake ballots, right? Just get out there and vote, or if you have an absentee, send it in. But there's nothing like getting out and voting. I did it two days ago and it was so good, I even got an 'I Voted' label and stuck it on my forehead, like when people mark their heads for Ash Wednesday.

Voting in person is great because there's no way you can cheat, unless you have a fake I.D. that says you're John Smith who died last year. Mail-in ballots are even worse. You don't know who's sending them. It could be some Autocrat flunky collecting hundreds of ballots then putting the names of people who don't even vote on them. It's ridiculous. It opens the door to massive fraud and insects.

All over the country, you're seeing liberal city officials illegally changing the voting rules to benefit Autocrats. Thousands and thousands of early ballots could be fraudulent. How about the military ballots that were thrown into a garbage can from people who voted for me? Oh, there's no voting fraud they swear. Ha!

Let me talk about Pennsylvania for a moment. Joe Hiden is a diehard globalist who wiped out your steel mills. You know it better than almost any place in this country. He closed down your factories, killed your coal jobs, outsourced your industries to China and supported every terrible and disastrous trade deal in the Obahma administration.

Joe enthusiastically voted for China's entry into the WHO, decimating your manufacturing and enriching China. Pennsylvania lost almost 50% of its manufacturing jobs after Joe's China debacle. Tired Joe has betrayed Pennsylvania. How the hell can you vote for him?

At the debate, he almost got through it without showing his true colors, black and white like a skunk. We have about a hundred clips, but we're only going to play a few of them for you now. This screen cost us a fortune so I hope you enjoy it."

Some video clips of the debates were then shown on a large screen.

Joe Hiden: "I'm supporting NAFTA because I think it is a positive thing to do. And I don't pretend to be an expert on international trade matters as many of you know. Ha. Ha."

Moderator: "When Obahma ran for President, you

Chapter 14

both said you would renegotiate NAFTA. You didn't. Trade agreements like NAFTA and permanent normal trade relations with China, forced American workers to compete against people who were making pennies an hour. That resulted in the loss of 160,000 jobs."

Joe Hiden: "You don't understand. I call it the China awakening and it is an incredibly positive development for not only China, but the United States and the rest of the world. Trading with China is a positive, positive development like one end of a car battery. If you put your hands on both terminals you'll get one hell of a shock, but... where am I going with this? Anyway, it is in my, I mean *our* self-interest that China continues to prosper. China's a great nation and we should hope for its continued expansion in the Pacific, Atlantic, Indian, Arctic, and Southern Oceans. China is not our enemy, contrary to what all the experts say. China isn't even our competitor. We should be helping them by sharing all our secrets and intellectual property. The idea that China is going to eat our lunch when most of them don't even like American food is bizarre. Come on, man. They're not bad folks, folks. Hey, they've paid my son Bunter a lot of money so you can't say they're not contributing to my, uh, our economy. China's not a problem. We're the problem. Just give them a few trade deals and they'll reciprocate... I'm sure they will eventually."

Moderator: "Allowing China into WHO, which you supported, and extending most favored nation status to China, which you also supported, those steps allowed China to take advantage of the United States by using our own open trade deals against us. Do you think in retrospect that you were naive about China?"

Hiden: "C'mon man."

Moderator: "You have said you oppose fracking..."
Hiden: "I have never said I oppose fracking."
Trumpet: "You said it on tape."
Hiden: "I did. I don't remember saying that."
Trumpet: "You don't remember a lot of things. I'll put it on my website."
Moderator: "Mr. Hiden . Would there be any place for fossil fuels, including coal and fracking, in a Hiden administration?"
Hiden: "No, we would make sure it's eliminated. I guarantee you we're going to end fossil fuels. No more. No new fracking. I'll gradually move away from fracking and pracking."
Moderator: "What's pracking?"
Hiden: "It's a new word I just made up. I like to make up things."

The tape then switched to the debate between Camela Heiress and Mike Pensive.

Moderator: "What's your view on fossil fuel leases?"
Heiress: "Ha, ha, ha, ha. I think it's critically important on day one that we end any fossil fuel leases on public lands."
Moderator: "But what about, say, stopping fracking and stopping pipeline infrastructure."
Heiress: "Ha, ha, ha, ha, ha. There's no question I'm in favor of banning fracking. What was the other thing? Ha, ha, ha, ha, ha."

The tape then switched back to the Trumpet/Hiden debate.

Trumpet: "Joe said he would close down the oil industry."
Hiden: "No, I would *transition* from the oil industry to wind, solar, and hamster wheels."

Chapter 14

Trumpet: "Basically what he's saying is he is going to destroy the oil industry. Will you remember that Texas? Will you remember that Pennsylvania, Oklahoma?"

The tape ended and Trumpet continued with his speech to the Allentown crowd.

"That's why I brought all that expensive equipment because it's more effective than me just saying it, right?

And borders? We're going to defend our borders. Autocrats don't want to have borders. They want to have open borders so everybody and their drugs can get in. The wall I've been putting up is almost complete. Then we'll have the strongest border we've ever had. If you don't have borders, you don't have a country and if you don't have a country, you don't have, uh, hamburgers."

A chant rose up. "Build that wall. Build that wall. Build that wall. Build that wall. Build that wall."

Thank you. Yep. Very shortly it's going to be finished. We just hit 400 miles. Oh boy, that's a lot. And this is a wall that's exactly what border patrol and all of the law enforcement people wanted, not to mention the people that live in Texas, New Mexico, and Arizona.

The Autocrats say, "Walls are obsolete." I say, "No walls and wheels will never be obsolete. Walls and wheels and hamburgers." Everything else is going to be obsolete. And we want to ensure that more products are proudly stamped with the phrase, 'Made in the USA,' right?

We are going to deliver record prosperity, epic job growth... in fact, we're doing it already. 11.4 million jobs over the last few months. There's never been a time in our history where we put that many people to work that quickly. Groundbreaking therapies and safe vaccines that will end the pandemic are coming. We're rounding the turn. The vaccines being developed are going to be incredible. They'll be here soon. If somebody else were President, you'd get a vaccine in about forty years from now. Normal life, that's what we want, right. Normal life and hamburgers. And next year will be the greatest economic year in the history of our country. I gave working families record-setting tax cuts and Tired Joe's running on tax increases. He says it's just the rich but he keeps changing the numbers. Pretty soon it will be anyone who makes over $20,000 a year.

Did anybody see the program on TV last night with Camela Heiress? She kept laughing while being interviewed and I said, 'Is there something wrong with her? Somebody off camera must be tickling her feet or something.' She kept laughing at very serious questions. And then did you see the interview with Joe? It was so soft. The phony media is trying to protect him. He's walking out of a shop with ice cream and a reporter asked, "Mr. Vice President, what flavor is the ice cream?"

He replied, "It's vanilla and chocolate with viagra sprinkles."

I don't get easy questions like that, right. I get questions like, "How come you're such a racist, xenophobic, misanthropic, transphobic, puppy killer."

Did you like all the regulations under Obahma and Hiden ? Tired Joe wants to put back all the restrictive government regulations their administration created, which were terrible. It would take 20 years to get a golf course approved, 50 years to get a parking lot approved, and 100 years to get a conservative rally approved!

So your liberal officials here didn't want us to have a site for our rally. No freedom of speech, right. And these are the people who are counting your votes. So be very vigilant and watch the voting polls. Did you see where

Chapter 14

they fought us because they didn't want poll watchers? They took us to court and the judge said, "You can't have poll watchers." So he's saying we can't even watch as they count the ballots, but we're going to appeal it. Can you believe it? Autocrats don't want people watching them count the votes. Now why would they object to people verifying that the votes are counted properly? Could it be because they want to CHEAT!

If Tired Joe and his Autocrat socialists are elected, they will delay the vaccine, delay therapies, prolong the pandemic, close your schools, and shut down all the burger and pizza joints. All the world leaders don't want to deal with Tired Joe. One of them said to me, "Well, I hope you win because we don't want to deal with somebody that takes naps all the time." I think Joe hates unscripted appearances because he can't answer questions without a cheat sheet, then he forgets which pocket it's in.

When these pea brains in the news media ask him questions, he can't answer the simplest one. How about where they gave him questions on a teleprompter? They said, "Here are the questions." And they wrote out the answers for him. And then social media closes down anybody that goes against their progressive propaganda.

They banned *The New York Posts* newspaper from being on *Mugbook* and *Tooter*. Can you believe it, *The New York Posts*? In an interview that aired last night, Tired Joe said he opposes letting young, unvaccinated Americans resume their lives, even though most are at extremely low risk, 99.99%. Now as an example, I had the virus and here I am. My wife had it and she's fine. Baron had it and he's fine because kids have a stronger immune system and they won't let anything stop them from playing video games. 99.98% of those under the age of 50 fully recover. But Tired Joe wants to keep the whole country on lockdown, keep them in their homes while letting rioters and looters run wild. He calls them peaceful protesters when they're beating up reporters and setting fires. Actually, the only thing you can do in Pennsylvania is protest. You can't go to church. You can't be with your pastors, your priests, or your rabbits. You can't do anything. You can't go shopping. You can't open your stores, you can't even pick your nose without wearing disposable gloves. But if you want to riot and burn the hell out of your city, no problem, you can do that. That's okay.

When the China virus arrived we banned travel from China and Europe. Tired Joe didn't want to. He said, "Oh, you shouldn't do that. You're xenophobic." Right. He called me racist. He called me everything in the book. That was in January. Two months later, he said, "Trumpet should have done it earlier." Same with Lugosi. When the virus was just starting to spread, she was dancing in the streets with crowds of people late at night in China Town. Nightstalker Nancy I called her. Then she changed her mind and said everyone should social distance and wear a mask. Shortly after that, she goes to the beauty parlor without a mask. What a hypocrite.

My administration has brought in medical supplies, ventilators, built hospitals from scratch, slashed red tape, and pioneered groundbreaking therapies. I wish the governor in New York would have used the convention center and the big hospital ship I sent him for seniors. Did he use it? No. It sat there practically empty all the time. If he would've used the ship and the convention center for COBID cases, you would have had a lot more rest home seniors in New York who survived the pandemic.

Chapter 14

We reduced the fatality rate, 85%. Think of that. That's because of what we've come up with over the last little while. So when this pandemic first hit, the media was projecting that it could be as bad as 2.2 million deaths. Now we have therapies, therapeutics, the vaccines are coming and I really think we saved 2 million lives. The phony news will never say that. And we will deliver 100 million doses of a safe vaccine before the end of the year.

Most importantly, we're protecting the elderly and those with underlying conditions. Keeping this virus from spreading has been my top priority from the beginning. China wants Tired Joe to win because they own him. They own his son Bunter too. He never made 25 cents in his life, then all of a sudden Bunter Hiden is making millions of dollars a year from Ukrane and China. Unbelievable. And Joe got 10% according to an email and the press doesn't want to talk about it?

Ladies and gentlemen, newsflash. I just found out that Tired Joe will be doing a lid today which means he's either smoking a joint or taking a break from the campaign trail for a week. If he's taking a break, does that mean he's going to have a nap until then?

You got the Autocrats, you got the phony news media, and you have big tech. They're all partners for Hiden. And then you have the RHINOS-the bad Rebubbacans who are really Autocrats in conservative clothing.

In the last election, the Autocrats said I will not get the women's vote. And then at the end of the evening, you remember how great I did. Right? One of my best groups were women.

On CNN a broadcaster said, "Trumpet will not receive the women's vote. You know, Jim, this should be over very quickly." The end of the evening, they said,

"Man, did he do well with the women vote? What the hell happened?"

And then Tired Joe's going to pack the Supreme Court with radical justices who will shred your second amendment and pro-life. I have a list of 45 great people who believe in a thing called the Constitution. Joe believes in a thing called the Communist Manifesto.

Joe is a corrupt politician. He wants to destroy your energy jobs in Pennsylvania while his own son collected $183,000 a month for doing nothing at a Ukranian Energy Company. He also got three and a half million dollars from the wife of the mayor of Moscow. What the hell did he do for that? I'm not even going to speculate. He had no income, no job, no nothing until Joe was in the White House. Then he gets $1.5 billion to manage from China along with everything else.

Did you hear where he leaves his laptop at a repair store and forgets about it? The owner finds some material on it that ties Joe in a quid pro quo with China for money. Not only is he involved with a quid pro quo from Ukrane, but with China too. Some of the contents were published in *The New York Posts*. Social media refused to run the story and the left-leaning mainstream claimed they had no proof Joe Hiden was involved in the scandal. But we do. We have all kinds of proof on the laptop. But then they come up with a new excuse. It was Russian disinformation. Here we go, again. Three years of weaselly-faced Adam Shifty claiming I'm a Commie wasn't enough. Joe even said, "I believe that the laptop was created by Russia."

The Autocrats spent $48 million to bury the 'Laptop from Hades' that Bunter brought in to be fixed. That was a very expensive repair job, wasn't it? It was the second greatest crime in the history of our country. And the first was we caught them spying on my campaign. It was a treasonous act and we caught them. Unfortunately, we have people that don't want to expose bad publicity about Joe before the election because it might affect the results in my favor. It's okay to smear me, but it's not okay to do it to Joe.

If Joe wins, China wins. And if China has anything to do with it, they will own the United States of America.

I don't think China likes me much. I put a 25% tariff on their steel and your steel companies started doing well again."

Cheers from the crowd.

"Tired Joe said, "One of the first things I will do is take the tariffs off." Do you think China would like to see him get elected? If I don't sound like a typical Washington politician, it's because I'm not. If I don't always play by the rules of the Washington establishment, it's because I was elected to fight for you not the politicians."

The crowd cheered, "Four more years! Four more years!"

"Under my leadership, we achieved the most secure border in United States history. My opponents insane immigration plan would eliminate U.S. borders entirely by implementing nationwide catch and release. You know what catch and release is. Border patrol catches them, whether they're a murderer, or a rapist, or gang member then releases them into our country.

Joe at the debate said, "No, no it's okay because they come back for court." Nobody comes back. I ended catch and release because I didn't like catching a murderer and releasing them. Now we keep them out. You can come into our country, but you have to come in legally and you have to come in through merit. Joe's plan would also make every community into a sanctuary city. The Hiden/Heiress plan would also increase refugees coming into our country by more than 700%. It would be the highest level anywhere in the world. They wanted to terminate all national security travel bans, opening the flood gates to radical Islamic terrorism. I'm keeping the terrorists, jihadists, violent extremists, and leprous pedophiles the hell out of our country. Is that okay?

Cheers from the crowd.

"And I just got a 91% approval rating from our veterans, the highest ever. Remember for years you'd always see how badly vets were treated. Before I became President, it would take weeks before a vet could see a doctor. Now they can go to a private doctor and the government pays the bill. Nobody thought we could do that but we did.

I withdrew from the last administration's disastrous Iran Nuclear Deal. One of the stupidest deals ever. This was John "Hari" Keri's brilliant brainthrust. The Obahma Administration paid $1.8 billion in cash for an agreement by the Iranians not to build nuclear weapons. Hello. What do you think nuclear weapons plants make? Diapers?

Instead of never ending Wars, I am forging peace in the Middle East. I'm going to bring our soldiers and all the figs they can carry back from Afghanistan. I happen to like fig newtons.

In conclusion, over the next four years I will make America the manufacturing superpower of the world and we will end our reliance on China once and for all. It's already happening. I will hire more police, increase penalties for assaults on law enforcement, and I will ban sanctuary cities and clowns. Clowns scare the hell out of me.

I will uphold religious liberty, free speech and the right to keep and bare your arms and legs. I will maintain

Chapter 14

America's unrivaled military might by giving our troops free gym passes and steroids.

Autocrats want to keep everything shut down, but I want to open businesses back up before it's too late and they all go out of business except for the online stores.

I will ensure peace through strength. I will maintain American energy independence. I will end surprise medical billing parties, require price transparency, and lower drug prices even more for our senior citizens and raising them for the drug cartels.

I will stop the radical indoctrination of our students and restore patriotic education to our schools. I will teach our children to love our country, honor our history, and always respect our great American flag. We will live by the timeless words of our national motto, "In God We Trust, All Others Pay Cash." The left wanted to take out the words, 'One nation, under God' out of our Pledge of Allegiance, but I put it back in to say 'under God and

Donald Trumpet.'"

Crowd: "God loves Trumpet!"

"Yes, He does. For the last four years, you have seen me fight for you, and now I am relying on you to deliver another historic victory for our country. On November 3rd, we must finish the job and drain the marsh and the creatures in it once and for all.

Crowd: "Whoop! Whoop!"

There have never been rallies like this. We were in Ohio, Wisconsin, and yesterday we were in New Hampshire. They were the biggest rallies that anyone's ever seen. Wherever we go we have tens of thousands of people. There's never been anything like that before.

Tired Joe goes out and four people show up. He's drawing flies and crickets. Now nobody's going because Joe keeps hidin' in his basement. Get it? Hidin' Hiden?

Now the phony news is tormented. They have to keep their cameras on at my rallies because it means ratings. In another way, CNN hates when I say CNN is phony corrupt news so they'll cut that part out. Anytime I say something they don't like, they say, "Now let's go to a commercial break." They're tormented because they want the ratings. Without coverage of me, they get terrible ratings. They want the ratings, but at the same time, they don't want to be talked about in a bad manner, right? But I have to talk about it because they're corrupt. They're the enemy of the people, puppies, and kittens.

Proud citizens like you helped build this country. Together we are taking back our country. We are returning power to you, the American people. With your help, your devotion, and your drive, a little golf analogy there, we are going to keep on working. We are going to keep on fighting, and we are going to keep on winning!"

Chapter 14

The crowd roars.

"We have made America strong again. We have made America proud again. We have made America safe again, and we will make America terrific again. Thank you, Pennsylvania. Now go out and vote, you Steelers."

CHEERS!

The song "Allentown" by Billy Jole blares over the loudspeakers.

Late that night Trumpet Tooted: *Had a great rally in Pennsylvania. If the voting is conducted fairly, there's no doubt in my mind we will win a second term. The only things I'm afraid of are voter fraud and snakes.*

Chapter 15
Lying's and Censors and Snakes... Oh My!

It was evident from the very beginning that the deck was stacked against Trumpet being re-elected. *Mugbook, Tooter,* and other liberal social media platforms also played major roles in swaying the election. They refused to run any pro-Trumpet posts and only displayed pro-Hiden posts. Anyone who posted any derogatory remarks about Joe Hiden had their comments removed and in many cases, their profiles. Not only did they censor all conservative posts on their platforms including Trumpet himself, they also allowed anti-Trumpet posts from liberals and Chinese government agents who were especially against Trumpet because of the strict tariffs he had placed on China for unfair trade practices. The Bunter Hiden "Laptop from Hades" story only made it to *The New York Posts* and when they tried to put it on social media, it was immediately removed. Pay no attention to the photos and videos of Bunter Hiden participating in drug use and pornography, or the verified emails sent by him that implicated Joe in shady financial deals. Social media was like the Wizard of Ozz and the American public was Dorothy. The wizards of social media only wanted Dorothy to see what they wanted her to see.

No doubt, the pandemic turned out to be an Achilles heel for Trumpet and the progressive news media kept shooting arrows in it.

Chris Madviews on MSNBC reported:

"Well, it's obvious that our President hasn't managed this pandemic very well. Thousands of Americans have died thanks to his poor decisions. I feel sorry for

Chapter 15

his virus management team who have had to implement all his orders which have resulted in catastrophe for the American people. If only he had listened to Tony Fowchi's recommendations, nobody would have died. That's the problem with having a dictator in the White House."

Unfortunately, Fowchi was as undecisive as a contestant on *The Price Is Right?* Trumpet did listen to his proposals at first, but after awhile, Fowchi's recommendations seemed confusing and in some cases contrary to what the President was saying.

Here are some of Fowchi's greatest hits:
"Don't worry about the virus, baby."
"Travel bans will keep us apart. No, no, no!"
"COBID-19 is only as bad as the flu, Lou."

Another strike against Trumpet occurred at the first debate with an exchange he had with Hiden that raised definite red flags with progressives and independents.

Trumpet: "I spoke with the scientists working on a vaccine for the pandemic and they assured me they will have a vaccine very soon."

Hiden : "With all the lies the President has told the American people, do you believe for one minute he's telling you the truth?"

Trumpet: "Joe doesn't even know the meaning of the word truth. I *have* spoken with the companies working on the vaccine and they said we could have the vaccine sooner if Autocrats and the press that supports them quit making the issue political and were more interested in saving lives. They said they might even have a vaccine before November."

November? That was the month to vote. The Autocrats couldn't have an effective vaccine distributed before election month. That would give Trumpet a giant feather in his *Dare To Be Terrific* cap.

Pressure was put on the vaccine manufacturers to slow down development by Autocrats and their minions. Hiden and Heiress also did their part in casting doubt on any vaccine endorsed by Trumpet. The problem as the Autocrats saw it, was that the vaccine wasn't going through months and even years of testing, which was the usual procedure. But because the virus was so deadly, especially for the elderly and people with existing conditions, Trumpet encouraged the vaccine companies to speed up the process, calling it "***Operation Light Speed***."

In the final months before the election, anti-Trumpet commercials filled with false information flooded the airwaves financed by the very pharmaceutical companies that were working on the vaccine.

To make matters worse for Trumpet, the FDA declined to approve the vaccine or any promising therapeutics that could be used against the virus until after the election. The bottom line is that the vaccine and effective therapeutics could have easily been distributed before the election, but the tentacles of the Autocratic octopus made sure they weren't released until it was advantageous for Hiden's win. After all the misleading information put out about the efficacy of the vaccine, only 50% of the American people trusted it. Especially after Camela Heiress said in her debate with Mike Pensive, "If Dr. Fowchi tells me I should take the vaccine, I'll take it. But if Donald Trumpet tells me to take it, I'm not taking it."

The New York Grimes ran an opinion piece that said: *"Trumpet's dangerous obsession with a hasty vaccine could jeopardize the safety of all Americans and could lead to the deaths of millions. It would destroy public confidence in vaccines forever and cause vaccineophobia."*

The newspaper failed to note that practically every vaccine produced had a high failure rate, even when they had been thoroughly tried and tested in accordance with all the standards established.

Brian "Alka" Seltzer on CNN said: *"If the vaccine is rushed, the likely result of October vaccinations will be deadly fevers, migraine headaches, and in many cases, your arm falling off."*

The President of CNN, Jeff Zooker, had made it clear to all the on-air commentators at the station, that they were to "make sure Donald Trumpet is not elected no matter what you have to embellish or invent." In essence, "Toe the anti-Trumpet line or you're fired."

On November first, Trumpet boarded Air Force One for his few last campaign stops. Corey Looseandrowsy, Dave Bossy, Jared Kushyner, and other campaign advisers were also on the plane.

Bossy gave everyone on board a concerned look and prophetically stated, "You had better be prepared for what is coming on election day."

The blood drained from Looseandrowsy's face and he said, "You think we'll be attacked by zombies?"

Bossy exhaled a deep breath and replied, "Worse. I think the Autocrats will attack our voting procedures and rig the results for their benefit."

Kushyner, however, waved his hands and shook his head like the election was in the bag and began to sing, "Everything is beautiful."

Bossy wasn't hearing it, since he was standing next to a speaker that started playing another Eldon John song at full volume. He shouted, "I don't know what you said, Jared, but you had better take this election seriously. These Autocrats with their unscrupulous methods can steal the whole enchilada and make it look legal."

Kushyner patted him on the head like he was his pet dog and said, "We'll be fine, Dave. Besides, I hate enchiladas. The Autocrats can have them."

Stepping away from the speaker, Bossy sighed and continued. "I was a chief investigator for Congress and you don't know these Autocratic snakes like I do. I don't think you guys are ready for what's coming."

On the last day of the trip, everyone on the plane was congratulating themselves on a great campaign while Corey Looseandrowsy sang, "For he's a jolly good fellow," again. This time Trumpet let him sing.

The polling data indicated that the Trumpet campaign was in better shape than his first, so no one seemed too concerned, except Bossy.

Rebubbacan campaign workers had knocked on more doors and sent out more online reminders to vote than bugs on every car windshield in the south. A Trumpet second term seemed inevitable, like Bunter Hiden starring in his own porno movie.

In a New Hampshire town hall meeting, a voter asked Joe why she should trust him to turn his campaign

Chapter 15

around after he had spent so much time off the campaign trail.

Joe asked if she's ever been to a caucus before and the girl said "Yes." Joe shocked her and the crowd by saying, "No you haven't. You're a fibbing canine-countenanced horse trooper."

One of the secret service agents with him turned to another and asked, "What did he say?"

"Don't bother, just make sure you grab an arm if he starts to fall."

Then Joe gave a short monlogue that went as follows: "I just want to say how good it feels to be back here in Illinois..." turning to an aide who whispered something, he said, "What? Oh, I mean New Hampshire. I should know that, I was born here." His aide whispered to him again. Joe chuckled and said, "I mean I was born not too far away from here. Anyway, when I was a kid, I helped keep the streets safe from thugs like Pop Corn and his gang of midgets..." His aide whispered to him again. "What? Oh, I mean little people. And if I'm elected President, I promise to keep you safe again and get the white, right wing criminals off America's streets!"

He received a smattering of applause.

Then came the day when the polls closed and the returns started coming in. TV screens were scattered all around the East room and the aroma of hamburgers, chicken tenders, and french fries hung in the air like stale cigarette smoke. Nervous chatter filled the room sounding like wind-up plastic teeth, and a pizza delivery guy looked around frantically for someone to pay him for the fifty extra large pizzas somebody had ordered.

By midnight, things were looking good for Trumpet. Steve Cannon even reported on his podcast from the rooftop of a building on Constitution Avenue saying, "We've got this!"

The next morning, Steve Cannon called Pete Navarho and bellowed, "They stole the election!"

****

Navarho wasn't about to let the Autocrats get off that easy. He went to work and found anomalies in the voting results which raised questions about the legitimacy of the election. He also had questions regarding the halting of vote counts, harvested bundled votes with questionable origins, and Rebubbacan poll watchers not being allowed to observe the vote counts in some battleground states. The states in question were Arizona, Georgia, Michigan, Nevada, Pennsylvania, and Wisconsin. He researched hundreds of election irregularity reports from the six battleground states and found evidence of the following: ballot mishandling, process fouls, Equal Protection Clause violations, voting machine irregularities, statistical anomalies, bribery, fake ballots, ballots counted multiple times, no voter ID checks, and ineligible voters that included dead and ghost voters. Wisconsin was especially egregious when it came to voting violations. They set up drop boxes in heavily Autocratic areas, which was illegal as well as backdating ballots which was also against the state law. As many as 100,000 ballots were backdated. Navarho compiled all these anomalies and presented them to Trumpet.

When Trumpet sought legal help to file lawsuits regarding these questionable procedures, Rebubbacan law firms turned their backs on him and threatened to fire or cancel any attorney in their employ who offered their services. He found snakes in the Rebubbacan side of the marsh too.

Chapter 15

To show just how powerful the cancel culture snakes were, the Texas attorney general filed a case before the U.S. Supreme Court alleging that four states-Georgia, Michigan, Pennsylvania, and Wisconsin had ignored federal and state election laws using the pandemic as an excuse, thereby disenfranchising Texas voter results. They contended that Hiden winning the popular vote in those four states was about as probable as Vladimir Pootin carrying those states.

The expert witness who was brave enough to file the brief was pummeled by the anti-Trumpet press and Autocrat elites like a conservative reporter surrounded and beaten by ANTIFA thugs. It was a warning to others who wanted to pursue investigating the election to back off or suffer the consequences. Those close acquaintances surrounding Trumpet thought it better to just concede the election and look to 2024 for a comeback.

Autocratic secretaries of state for Michigan and Pennsylvania, funded by George Souros-the socialist/Marxist globalist, also played key roles in election misconduct. They abolished signature analysis for absentee and mail-in ballots which allowed thousands of questionable ballots to be cast which should not have been, according to the state laws. But the laws were ignored by the very officials who were supposed to enforce them. Social media and the progressive press posted only favorable ads and comments for Hiden but wouldn't post favorable ads and comments for Trumpet, only unfavorable ones. It was like all the adverse weather elements came together to form a perfect storm for the Autocrats. In this case, the perfect storm was Hurricane Hiden and Trumpet could only cry foul.

Trumpet Tooted: If an Autocrat Presidential Candidate had an election rigged & stolen, with proof of such acts at a level never seen before, the Autocrat Senators would have investigation after investigation, and never give up. McColonel & the Rebubbacans aren't going to do anything to contest this swindle of the American people. What a travesty of justice.

Chapter 16
The Final Nail in the Coffin

After the election, Trumpet met with his closest allies, namely his son Donny Jr., Jared Kushyner, Corey Looseandrowsy, David Bossy, and other loyal pro-Trumpeters to plan their next course of action.

As Trumpet's supporters sat around the large corporate table, their expressions were a mix of anger and disbelief.

"What the hell happened?" Trumpet bellowed.

"I told these guys to be prepared for election day but nobody listened to me," Bossy commented, then gave Jared Kushyner a scowl when Kushyner threw a *Make America Terrific Again* hat at him.

"Well, we can't let these guys steal the presidency," Trumpet blared. "I won the election and everyone knows it. The only way Hiden won is by cheating and from what I've been told, we have plenty of evidence to prove it."

Pete Navarho stood up and said, "That's right, Mr. President. Just so everyone here is aware, I have binders of proof and testimonies of solid witnesses who swear there was fraudulent activity in several of the battleground states."

Trumpet nodded and said, "Pete did a great job of tracking all the illegal actions the Autocrats pulled during the election which proves without a doubt that the election was a fraud. Thanks, Pete."

Navarho puffed out his chest like a bullfrog's chin and sat down.

"What can we do now, Dad?" Donny Jr. asked. "They're counting the electoral votes tomorrow."

"Well, there's the *Save the U.S.A.* rally tomorrow at the Ellipse," Bossy stated. "About the only thing we can do is appeal to the pro-Trumpet protesters to seize and destroy all the electoral votes in the Capitol and have every state do a recount with Rebubbacan watchers to verify the results."

"But that would result in a clash between protesters and the police, who will certainly be positioned around the Capitol to prevent just that," Looseandrowsy commented.

"I don't want violence, that would just delegitimize our cause," Trumpet said, rubbing his forehead.

"Well, from some of the social media posts I've read, there's going to be violence anyway," Donny Jr. reported. "I've been watching some of these far right group posts like the Proud Guys and QAnone and they favor an armed insurrection."

"Absolutely not," Trumpet said, with a definitive

Chapter 16

scowl. "I'm not going to have the phony press accuse me of orchestrating an insurrection."

"I think that's what they're going to say anyway, no matter what happens, Dad," Donny Jr. added. "All we can hope for is that nobody brings their AR-15's or Glocks."

"Have you seen some of the posters people are carrying promoting violence?" Kushyner asked. "Some say 'Off With The Autocrats Heads,' 'Lugosi is Satan' and 'Jesus Loves Rebubbacans.' What if the rally turns into a riot and the people go after the politicians in the Capitol?"

"I think the Capitol Police will make sure the politicians will be safe if things get out of hand," Trumpet remarked. "Let's just hope they don't or things could get real ugly for us in the news."

"Then you may as well forget seizing the electoral votes," Bossy stated.

Navarho shook his head and said, "So we're back to square one."

"Then we're doomed," Looseandrowsy stated before putting his head down on the table and falling asleep.

"If I have to take this travesty all the way to the Supreme Court, then that's exactly what I'll do!" Trumpet announced, pounding his fist on the table.

This startled Looseandrowsy, who reared up like a man who had just been goosed.

"Good luck," Bossy said under his breath.

The next day, the *Save The USA* rally took place in the Ellipse within the National Mall just south of the White House. Thousands of Trumpet supporters gathered to hear speeches from Trumpet, Rudy Jeweliani, and others. Mo Betta Brooks was a featured speaker at the rally and said, "Today is the day American patriots start taking butts and kicking names. Are you willing to fight for America?"

"Yeah!" the crowd screamed.

"Louder! Will you fight for America?"

"YEAH!"

Trumpet's sons also spoke, criticizing Rebubbacan congressmen and senators who were not supporting the effort to challenge the Electoral College vote, and promising to campaign against them in future primary elections and not validate their parking tickets. There were also calls for Mike Pensive and Congress to reject Hiden's victory for religious reasons.

Trumpet delivered his rally speech from behind a bullsh#%-proof shield, projected onto a large screen and declared he would "never concede" the election. He also criticized the media, and called for Pensive to overturn the election results. He didn't overtly call on his supporters to use violence or enter the Capitol, but suggested that his supporters had the power to prevent Hiden from taking office if they convinced him the White House was being renovated and wouldn't be finished for another four years.

Trumpet also called for the people to go to the Capitol and demand that Congress only count the electoral votes from states that conducted their voting lawfully. He then listed a dozen who didn't, including Venezuela which he just threw in to make a point.

During his speech, his supporters chanted "Storm the Capitol" and "Cobid masks are for sissies." Trumpet, however, admonished them to do things peacefully. Before he had finished speaking, an estimated eight thousand supporters had already begun moving up the National Mall, with some shouting that they were taking over the Capitol. After completing his speech, Trumpet went back to the White House on the Presidential motor-

Chapter 16

cade. At some point afterward, he went to the Oval Office and started watching news coverage of the demonstration. The news channels reported it as a day that would live in infamy, comparing it to Pearl Harbor.

Thousands of attendees walked to the Capitol and hundreds breached police perimeters, encouraged by agitators. One named Ray Oops, was particularly vocal, inciting people to riot and become violent. Strangely enough, although he was seen on several videos, he was never arrested. Some thought he was an agent of the government's progressive far left wing trying to turn a peaceful demonstration into a riot and make Trumpet supporters look like seditionists and domestic terrorists. It worked.

Congress was just beginning the electoral vote count during this time when more than 2,000 people broke into the Capitol building. Some assaulted police but most just wandered around. A few vandalized the office of House Speaker Nancy Lugosi and others, but only minor thefts and damage occurred. With building security breached, Capitol Police evacuated Senators and Representatives then locked down both chambers of Congress and several buildings in the Capitol Complex. A few protesters occupied the empty Senate chamber while federal law enforcement officers watched over the House floor. One unarmed protester was shot and killed by a Capitol Police officer when she tried to enter a barricaded room. The shooting was later ruled justified, even though she had no weapon and was not making a threatening move toward the officer other than trying to enter the room. A few other deaths resulted from the protest but all but one was due to natural causes, an investigation later discovered.

Several liberal news media outlets reported that

one Capitol police officer was bludgeoned with a fire extinguisher by a protester and transferred to the hospital where he died. It was later learned that the officer suffered a stroke and was never struck with a fire extinguisher.

Trumpet reasserted in a video that afternoon, that the election was "fraudulent." He Tooted: *"This is what happens when an obvious victory is illegally stripped away from patriotic voters who have been mistreated and abused by the Marsh for so long. Remember this day for as long as you live as the day your government cheated your right to elect who you want to lead you. Go home in peace... if the Autocrats will let you."*

The Capitol Police cleared all the protesters off the grounds by mid-evening, and the counting of the electoral votes resumed. It was completed in the early morning hours of January 7.

Mike Pensive declared President-elect Joe Hiden and Vice President-elect Camela Heiress victorious.

Trumpet later conceded the election in a televised statement. "A new administration will be inaugurated on January 20th. My focus now turns to ensuring a smooth, orderly and seamless transition of power, so I've ordered all the White House batteries be turned over to Hiden. This moment calls for healing and reconciliation that will require all of us to come together, right now, over me. To those of you who have been loyal supporters these past four years, I can only say our incredible journey is just beginning. As the old man declared when the body gatherers threw him on the 'dead' wagon in that Monty Piethon movie *The Holy Grill*, 'I'm not dead yet.' Thank you for letting me be myself and God bless."

Trumpet's *Tooter* and *Mugbook* profiles and all his supporters' profiles were immediately suspended from

Chapter 16

the social media platforms including any print media profiles that were considered pro-Trumpet. The media companies said it was just a glitch in their systems that they should have rectified within a year or two.

After Trumpet gave his concession speech, Nancy Lugosi called a meeting for all the Autocrats in the House of Representatives. Stepping up to the podium, an evil grin forced its way on her surgically reconstructed face as her sunken eyes popped out and danced around the room. Eventually, they returned and her gaze fixed on the House gavel. A thin line of drool escaped the corner of her mouth and her pulse quickened to 5 beats per minute. Picking up the small wooden hammer, she crashed it down hard on the sound block three times causing a shiver to go down her crooked spine. "Fellow Autocrats," she screeched like a Bornean Horseshoe Bat, "it is my extinct pleasure to announce that Donald Trumpet, that foul racist, disgusting homophobe, revolting misogynist, and crass white supremacist, who has plagued our sacrosanct political marsh four long years... is now... DEAD!"

A deafening roar thundered in the chamber and every Autocrat threw their blue hats they were given in the air that said, "Make America Trumpetless!"

Now they had to worry about Hiden's inauguration. What if Trumpet's domestic terrorists returned, but this time they brought weapons of mass destruction? Nancy Lugosi went into high gear to prepare for just such an eventuality. She hired construction workers who erected sections of tall fencing with razor wire and ballistic missiles all around the Inauguration site. Lugosi also called up the National Guard and ordered 25,000 troops to provide security. Since there were no facilities to house them, they were allowed to sleep in nearby hotel garages with no portable toilets.

"Hey, that's what latrines are for," Lugosi told them.

It only cost 2 billion dollars to repair the holes they dug... paid by the taxpayers, of course.

****

On CNN, Brian "Alka" Seltzer described the disorder at the Capitol as an "armed insurrection" since everyone had arms (except for one veteran who lost both of his during the war), and also called it an act of widespread domestic terrorism (although the large majority of demonstrators merely walked about like tourists and participated in no violence at all), and even a treasonous coup against the government.

Dr. Hop Sing of the Ponderosa Coup Studies and Cooking School disagreed since Trumpet did not order the military to seize power on his behalf. Trumpet did, however, order the cookbook written by Dr. Sing entitled, *The Strategy and Logic of Military Coups and Crowd Food Preparation*.

A former disgruntled member of Trumpet's cabinet described his actions as an attempted self-coup in that he was trying to overthrow himself.

Liz Chainy, a Rebubbacan who voted to impeach Trumpet, went on Foxy News and said: "We have to take a really hard look at who the Rebubbacan Party is and what we believe in. We should be more passive, apologize for our whiteness, and accept the Autocratic standard of democracy which is: "Accept our ideology or be destroyed." I think that when you look at Trumpet's actions leading up to the revolt at the capitol, you have to ask yourself, does a business man with no seedy political experience really belong in the White House? Sure, he's done a lot for the country while he was President, but

Chapter 16

he incited a riot by insisting the election was fraudulent when every woke person knows it wasn't. He was even impeached by some Rebubbacans who think *he's* revolting and cheats at miniature golf. The fact that he lost the presidency and Rebubbacans lost the Senate should tell you how the people feel about him. CNN reported his approval rating is now at -10 points according to a poll taken in their D.C. newsroom. The Rebubbacan Party needs to be in a position where we stand for principles and for ideals, like Wokeism and Critical Racist Theory. We should not be embracing the former President, we should be embracing our marsh compatriots across the aisle. We've had four years of divisive rhetoric… that's what we get for electing a divider for President. I have all the confidence in the world that Honest Joe Hiden will bring our country together."

****

The House passed a bill to create a bipartisan independent commission to investigate the January 6th demonstration, or as the Autocrats put it, "an attack on our democracy, our freedoms, and our right to punish others for the same things we do." To their dismay, it was blocked by Rebubbacans in the Senate for being obviously partisan, so the Autocratically controlled House approved a select committee with seven Autocrats and two Rebubbacans to investigate it instead. That seemed fair to Nancy Lugosi. She was quoted as saying, "Well, now that we've destroyed Trumpet, we can destroy his supporters. If it takes the rest of my career in politics I'll hunt down every one and drain their blood just like Trumpet said he would 'drain the marsh.' Heh heh heh."

Hiden thanked Nancy for the offer, but decided that he would have the FBI track down Trumpet's minions to make it less gory.

By February first, he had charged over a thousand people involved in the Capitol protest with federal crimes or DC offences even though the large majority of them had no known affiliation with extremist groups and most of the charges were for tresspassing. Some of the protesters languished in dungeon-like cells for over a year watching their hearings get postponed over and over again by Autocratic-appointed judges. The judges excuses were that they were too busy releasing criminals whose bail was posted by Black Lives Madder or whose bail had been waived altogether.

The Autocrats had sent a clear message: "Trumpet supporters, we're going to destroy you."

****

Donald Trumpet was impeached for the second time, one week before his term expired. Ten Rebubbacan representatives voted for the second impeachment, the most pro-impeachment votes ever from a President's party. This was also the first Presidential impeachment in which all majority caucus members voted unanimously for impeachment.

The House of Representatives adopted one article of impeachment against Trumpet for "incitement of insurrection", alleging that he had incited the January 6 attack of the U.S. Capitol. These events were preceded by numerous unsuccessful attempts by Trumpet to overturn the upcoming Presidential election, as well as his pushing of voter fraud conspiracy theories on his social media channels before they were deleted. A single article of impeachment charging Trump with "incitement of insurrection" against the U.S. government and "lawless action at the Capitol" was introduced to the House of Repre-

Chapter 16

sentatives. The article had more than 200 co-sponsors. The same day, House Speaker Nancy Lugosi gave Vice President Mike Pensive an ultimatum to invoke Section 4 of the 25th Amendment to assume the role of acting President within 24 hours, or the House would proceed with impeachment proceedings. Pensive refused in a letter to Pelosi the following day, arguing that "It would not be in the best interest of our Nation or consistent with our Constitution." Nevertheless, a House majority passed a resolution urging Pensive to invoke the 25th Amendment.

The House impeachment managers formally triggered the start of the impeachment trial by delivering to the Senate the charge against Trumpet. The nine managers walked into the Senate chamber led by the lead impeachment manager, who read the article of impeachment. The trial in the Senate was scheduled to start on February 9, but this time, the Chief Justice chose not to preside as he had done for Trumpet's first impeachment trial. Vermont Autocratic senator Patrick Leafy, presided instead.

At the trial, 57 senators voted "guilty", which was less than the two-thirds majority needed to convict Trumpet, and 43 senators voted "not guilty," resulting in Trumpet being acquitted of the charges.

And with that, Hiden and his Department of Injustice's stormtroopers hammered the final political death nail in Trumpet's coffin.

Or at least, they thought they did.

If you're into historical fiction novels on ancient Rome,
you'll like Rod Warren's Praetorian Series:
The Praetorian and the Emperor's List
The Praetorian and the Vipers
The Praetorian and the Emperor's Madness
Available on Amazon or IngramSpark.com

If you like comic strips about the beach,
check out Rod's online posts about a bunch
of zany kids living in a beach community
called Pickle Beach. Just log onto
www.picklebeachcomics.com

www.ingramcontent.com/pod-product-compliance
Lightning Source LLC
Chambersburg PA
CBHW051428290426
44109CB00016B/1472